Capsules
of
Optimism

By Marcel-M. Desmarais, O.P.

Translated by Sister Maria Regina, I.H.M.

JOSEPH F. WAGNER, INC., PUBLISHERS
53 Park Place, New York, N. Y. 10008

Foreword

You can become an optimist.

Yes! Optimism can be acquired.

Even if you are naturally inclined to see everything in somber colors, do not consider yourself a hopeless case. The practices here suggested will lead you more and more frequently to put on rose-tinted glasses.

Even though heavy trials overwhelm you, you must never feel that all is lost forever. From the materials salvaged from the shipwreck, you can rebuild your life in wondrous beauty.

Consequently, no unfavorable condition can prevent optimism from gladdening your soul.

Come on then; what are you waiting for?

Be quick! Adopt the rules prescribed:

(1) Take these capsules. You will find in them the redemptive message of Jesus in the Gospel, clothed in modern terms.

(2) Ask of our Lord the grace to draw from them the maximum of mental and spiritual strength for your mental and spiritual growth.

Come! To work!

Soon, very soon, you will become—or become again— an optimist.

FATHER MARCEL-M. DESMARAIS, O.P.

Contents

	Page
FOREWORD	3
Chapter I. LEARN TO SMILE	7
A Question of Life or Death	9
The Little Demons	10
Black and Rose	13
New Little Trifles	14
The Professional Smiler	16
Legs, Eyes, Ears	17
The Sleepy Monk	19
Like an Echo	20
We Have the Face Which We Deserve	22
An Unfortunate Man	23
Chapter II. CULTIVATE HOPE	25
Never Despair	27
Let Us Bloom Where God Has Planted Us	29
Make the Best of Things	30
You Are the Architect of Your Own Happiness	32
At the Latest . . . Day After Tomorrow	34
Too Naïve?	35
Providence—Not Death!	36
In the Presence of Our Shattered Dreams	38
About Nervous Depression	39
Know How to Bounce Back	41
Heroism in the Garb of Work	42
A Parable	44
Chapter III. MAKE A SUCCESS OF YOUR LIFE	47
First on Your Agenda	49
On Your Guard!	50
Good Luck and Bad Luck	52
How to Prepare for a Happy Marriage	54
To You, Newlyweds!	56
We Can Always Break Our Chains	57
Sleep Soundly	58

	Page
Cork or Compass?	60
Today, Let Us Concern Ourselves With Today	61
Nothing for Nothing	63
Is Crime a Disease?	64
A Force Too Often Unrecognized	65
Chapter IV. UNDERSTAND YOUTH	67
An Attitude of Welcome	69
When They Fall in Love	70
Inn or Home?	72
Uncontrollable!	74
Unintentional Executioners	75
Let Us Keep in Touch	77
The Little Boy, Insufferable But Charming!	78
A Great Man Prays for His Son	80
The Little Girl—Her Mystery	81
Pardon, My Son	82
Chapter V. STRENGTHEN YOUR HOME LIFE	85
Pay Whatever It Costs	87
Tact	88
The Compass and the Helm	90
Only One Life	91
An Ounce of Prevention Is Worth a Pound of Cure	93
"Ah! the Camels!"	95
Do Not Crush Your Adversary	96
A Locomotive and a Dog	98
Love and Maturity	100
A Proof of Love: A Check?	101
Fool?	103
That Man! Your Husband	104
I Love You ... You Love Me ... Agreed!	106
Chapter VI. SPREAD HAPPINESS!	109
Sowers of Optimism	111
Praise and Its Importance	112
Life Savers—All	114
A Very Little Candle	115
In the Season of Roses	117

	Page
Spiritual "Caboclos"	119
The First Step	120
As in the Story Books	122
God's Postmen	123
Initiation to Love	124
Chain Reaction	126
An Amateur Photographer	128
Poor Stumbling Will!	129
Chapter VII. SEE THE INVISIBLE	131
A Modern Parable	133
A Propos of a Slogan	134
One Way: Forward!	136
Have Confidence in Me!	137
How Beautiful That Will Be!	138
My Donalda	140
A Parable for Today	141
Red-Blooded Christians	143
Miracles Under Our Eyes	145
Rain and Sunshine	146
All's Well That Ends Well	148
Is Your Pastor Wrong?	149
Agreed!	151
Chapter VIII. INCREASE YOUR POWER	153
Duped! Ridiculed! Cheated!	155
An Accessory!	156
Addressed to the Grumblers	158
Always Good Weather	159
In the Midst of the Summer Vacation	160
Never Abandoned	162
Like Mushrooms	164
Prayer An Opiate? No!	165
An Islet of Silence	166
Dignity and Familiarity	168
Actresses and Preachers	169
An Unusual Englishman	170
Saint Therese of Montreal	172

I

Learn to Smile

A QUESTION OF LIFE OR DEATH

If you are not already an optimist, make an effort to become one as soon as possible. I would dare to suggest that on this attitude of mind hinges the question of spiritual life or death.

Have you noticed that the ill-tempered, the surly, the eternal malcontents are also, with rare exceptions, scandal-mongers, slanderers, and jealous persons? The happiness of others saddens them; the virtue of others angers them. Then they try to drag everybody down to their own level.

What particularly exasperates these pessimists is what they call their "bad luck." But how could they succeed? Their whining drives away all help, all collaboration. And their lack of self-confidence lessens the efficacy of their own efforts.

The optimist, on the contrary, keeps saying to himself, "I will succeed," and he almost always does succeed. His hope stimulates, mobilizes all the resources of his soul and even of his body. In fact, modern science teaches us that positive feelings even improve the functioning of the endocrine glands.

Furthermore, the optimist practices fraternal charity more easily; his general attitude inclines him to kindness, pardon, and understanding.

* * *

How does one become an optimist?

I shall content myself today with a single recipe: smile in the presence of the little vexations of life.

You have slept badly and you get up in an ill-humor— your tongue is thick. Is this such a great misfortune?

9

While you are dressing, force yourself to sing, to whistle. Or just smile!

You don't have time to eat a hearty breakfast, as you usually do? So much the better for your figure. Anyhow, smile!

One of the children breaks a saucer. Is a fit of anger on your part going to glue the pieces together again? Well, smile!

You miss the bus. Make the best of things. And smile!

A companion wounds your vanity. It may just be that his liver is not functioning well. So, smile!

You will notice persons around you begin to smile in their turn, for people, like mirrors, reflect our own feelings.

And I, I tell you as did our Lord: "Blessed are the meek, blessed are the gentle, for they shall possess the land."

THE LITTLE DEMONS

Do you remember the little song: *Everything Is Fine, Your Ladyship!* ?

Everything Is Fine, Your Ladyship!

Hello, hello James! What news?
I've been away two weeks and am
   telephoning you; what will I
   find when I return?

Everything is fine, your Ladyship,
Everything is fine.
However, I must tell you: we
    regret
A trifling occurrence—an incident,
A stupid accident: the death of
    your grey mare.
But aside from that, your Ladyship,
Everything is fine, everything is fine.

Hello, hello James! What's this
    news?
My grey mare has died today?
My faithful butler, tell me how
    this came about.

It's nothing at all, your Ladyship,
    it's nothing at all, everything is
    fine.
However, I must tell you: we
    regret a trifling occurrence.
She died in the fire that destroyed
    your stables.
But aside from that, your
    Ladyship,
Everything is fine, everything is
    fine.

In fact, all was going very badly and the poor Lady
was learning by degrees of her complete ruin.

Ordinarily, so many misfortunes do not overwhelm us
at the same time.

11

Nevertheless, it seems as if a legion of little demons is busy plaguing us just at the most inopportune moments.

Have you noticed, for example, that your shoelaces break when you are in a hurry and are already late?

When does your television set get out of order? Certainly not on the evenings when the programs would bore you to death, but in the very midst of the World Series.

Then, too, the motor of your car purrs like a contented kitten when you are near a service station. But to sputter and finally come to a stop, it seems to choose the little country roads, far away from any help.

Now what are you to do in such circumstances?

(1) Do not fall into a fit of rage and anger. You will accomplish nothing that way. On the contrary, you will only make the situation worse.

(2) Do not curse and swear; do not blaspheme. This would be a lack of respect for God, your Father in heaven. It would also be a lack of tact, and of good breeding, and would prove how poor your command of language is, how meagre your vocabulary.

(3) Keep calm. You will act more quickly and find the best way out of the difficulty.

(4) If you have the courage, regard the situation with humor. Joke about it. Laugh about it.

(5) If you are a hero, think in these moments of the good fortune, of the providential circumstances from which you have benefited without too much remarking them.

12

Finally, in the face of life's thousand and one contradictions, learn to say to yourself, "Better laugh than weep."

BLACK AND ROSE

I beg of you, be an optimist! Force yourself always to look for the beautiful side of things, persons, and events.

No doubt you know the classic story of the bottle of wine. Here is the bottle; it is half full. A pessimist comes along. He lifts his arms and he cries in a tragic tone, "Ah! What a disaster! There is only a half left!"

Then comes the optimist. Smiling, he says, "Ah! What good luck! There is still a half left!"

Two conflicting evaluations—one black, cheerless, the other rose colored, happy—each in reference to the same bottle and the same quantity of wine.

In your opinion, who has the better sense? Is it not the optimist? It is he, in any case, who reacts most positively and most constructively.

Does it happen that you sometimes gripe, whine, complain, are ill-tempered even about trifles, mere nothings? It happens to me and at such times, I am able to find no solution—no solution at all.

Why, for instance, bluster against unpleasant weather? Will the most vehement jeremiad change anything?

How much wiser to remain calm, repeating the adage: "After the rain, good weather."

Let us go on to a more serious problem still.

13

Perhaps you are angry with God because he has not granted you a favor for which you have been begging a long time. Stop a minute and consider. Our Lord has taught us that God is our Father—our Father in heaven.

If you have children, do you give them everything they ask for? For instance, if your four-year-old son wishes to play with a knife, do you let him do it? No, of course not, and that is because you love him. It is also because of your love for him that you take him to the doctor or the dentist.

It is because God loves you that He sometimes treats you harshly.

Try then, to see in your trials, as in everything else, the good side—that aspect of them to which great hope may be attached.

In brief, endeavor to be an optimist in everything, everywhere, always!

NEW LITTLE TRIFLES

Do you want to know, my little lady, where almost all of your misfortunes come from?

Simply from this: You cultivate pessimism and bitterness with morbid complacency.

I beg of you, change your way of thinking—and do it as soon as possible!

From now on, make an effort to enjoy the beautiful and good in life.

Instead of concentrating on your misfortunes and your grievances, linger over the memory of the happy moments in your life. Gather like precious stones all your little successes; gild your small trifles. Place these carefully in your memory and often enter into yourself to contemplate them.

The smile of a friend, the splendor of a sunny day, the knitting, every stitch of which you lovingly count, the amusing story you have just read, the smiles of a rosy baby—place all these little trifles, like inestimable treasures, in a secret corner of your soul and look at them often, saying to yourself: "After all, life does have some fine moments."

Stop hypnotizing yourself by the consideration of your misfortunes. Think rather, of your great good fortune.

Little by little, you will become a smiling optimist.

Then you will see people drawn to you. Are they not attracted by gaiety—like moths to the light?

"An excellent program," you say, "but how difficult to realize!" Actually, it's not as difficult as you think. Did not your recent efforts to lose weight demand severe sacrifices? If you have succeeded in that effort, why not undertake with confidence these psychological gymnastics—this frequent contemplation of your happy memories. You will find so many advantages in the plan.

THE PROFESSIONAL SMILER

How many false ideas we too often have on the subject of Saints!

We imagine, for instance, that the great friends of God are pessimists, kill-joys, candle-snuffers.

What a mistake!

At any rate, I myself have known a believer, truest of the true, who was a joyous man in the real spirit of the Gospel.

Even when poverty imposed on him a life of austerity, even when bedridden by illness, there was always a smile on his lips, except for brief periods during which the severity of his sufferings succeeded, for a few hours or a few days, in making him yield to physical prostration.

About ten years ago, I saw the reaction of this truly great Christian in particularly dramatic circumstances.

From one moment to the next, we were expecting his death. Fully conscious, he had received the last sacraments with deep faith. His wife and children were around his bed weeping. Between gasps which seemed to be those of his last agony, he succeeded in saying, "Have confidence, I am about to play a good trick on the doctors. . . . See, I am like an old Studebaker; I seem to be going backward, but I am going forward."

And indeed, contrary to all expectations; contrary to the diagnosis of the great specialists, he recovered. His cure truly astonished everybody.

Last year, that man became ill again and this time without any hope of recovery.

He had cancer and he knew it. But he trained himself to hold on to his courageous spirit and his good humor.

When pain tortured him and sedatives seemed no longer to be effective, he succeeded in saying as if joking, "It means so much less of Purgatory. I prefer to endure as much of it as possible on this side of eternity."

When he was about to receive Viaticum for his last voyage and the priest spoke to him of the possibility of dying, he replied, "You know I am not in a hurry . . . But if the good God wills it. . . ."

Finally, a few moments before his death he said to his priest-son, "I did not think it was so difficult to die with a smile."

These words, at once so human and so Christian, were his last words. He died on June 11, 1965.

And this gallant Christian was my father.

LEGS, EYES, EARS

Last summer at one of the concerts in the Chalet de la Montagne in Canada, I saw a lovely young girl with light hair—gold as the wheat in the month of August. She appeared so cheerful that I envied her happiness. After the last applause had died away, she waited for a companion to help her stand up and leave. Why? A few seconds later, moved and saddened, I noticed that both her legs were encased in braces.

Lord, pardon me when I complain. I have two strong limbs and I can go where I wish. The world belongs to me.

17

While the crowd was dispersing, I went to a restaurant to buy cigarettes. The clerk was so amiable that I stayed to chat with him for a few minutes. When I was about to leave, he said to me, "Thank you, Sir. I like to chat with people like you. . . . You have not noticed, perhaps, but I am blind."

*   *   *

The next day, at lunch time, I saw a little lad in a schoolyard who was watching the other children at play. After a few moments, I went over to him and asked, "Why are you staying here all alone? Go ahead and play with the others." The little fellow did not budge. He was deaf.

Lord, pardon me when I complain. I have ears which hear even the murmuring of the wind in the branches. The world belongs to me.

My legs, my eyes, my ears—what treasures! Thank you, Lord!

*   *   *

I meditated on these incidents and then, instead of drawing up a catalogue of my hurts and my weariness, I made a list of everything I so thoughtlessly enjoy.

Now, do as I did. All will go so much better.

THE SLEEPY MONK

Permit me to relate to you from memory a legend I once read in the writings of Louis Veuillot, the French journalist. I hope you will find it, as I did, amusing and inspiring.

*   *   *

There was once a monk, the victim of an unconquerable inclination to sleep.

Was this a disease? We do not know. Nine times out of ten, the unfortunate monk continued to sleep, even after the general signal for rising at five o'clock in the morning.

Now nature, which had made him such a good sleeper, had also made him a very good mechanic.

Without studies, without any notion of mathematics —merely by dint of thought and work, he succeeded in making a perfect clock. To the usual chimes he added a carillon which, alas, soon proved insufficient. With tenacity of purpose, the old monk added to it a blackbird, a rooster, and a drum.

At rising time all these mechanisms would go off and the monk would spring from his bed.

However, after awhile, it happened that when five o'clock came, the carillon chimed, the blackbird whistled, the cock crowed, the drum beat—and the monk snored on.

At any cost, the scandal must be remedied. As a religious he felt guilty; as a mechanic he felt humiliated. The Devil assumed the air of defiance toward both the religious and the mechanic.

19

Then the poor monk invented a board which at the appointed hour came down on his feet. He had reached the last stage in his sleep-killing projects, when he knew it was time for him to go to sleep forever.

Sleep? Ah, no! A fervent religious did not think such thoughts. In spite of his inclination to sleep, filled with confidence in the mercy of God, he cried, "Ah! I am awake at last!" These were his last words.

He was indeed awakening to eternal rest. Happy monk!

LIKE AN ECHO

The little fellow, eight years old, had just come into the house with a black eye.

Enraged, furious, he tells through his tears a rather confused story, but one in which it is clear that the whole responsibility for the quarrel comes from the mischief of a young neighbor.

The mother listens with sympathy while bathing the injured eye with an ice-cold towel. Having calmed the child, she makes him understand that it takes two to make a fight.

Then the mother completes the lesson in Christian morals by an experiment which the child will remember all his life.

She takes him outside and talks to him: "You see these mountains all around you? Pretend that they represent your little friend. Insult them; call them names!"

The child does as she tells him. But because of the echo, all the ugly words reverberate—bounce back like rubber balls thrown against a cement wall. And the child, in his turn, hears himself called "cheater," "squealer," etc.

Then his mother invites him to call out: "Good morning! Let us make up! Let us remain friends! Come, play!" And the echo repeats with fidelity the same pleasant words.

* * *

You will, perhaps, smile at my story. You realize however, that it illustrates an essential principle of human psychology.

Truly, the reactions of those around us almost always reflect, like an echo, our own conduct and attitudes. If at certain times those around us display bad humor, are hard to get along with, are pessimistic, it is often because we ourselves have adopted like attitudes.

Do you like to see your relatives and friends smile and be friendly toward you? Be kind, amiable, and optimistic yourself. In short, follow the Golden Rule given by Jesus: "Do unto others as you would have them do unto you."

WE HAVE THE FACE WHICH
WE DESERVE

You are beautiful or you are ugly, just as you may have blue eyes or you may have black eyes.

That is a situation about which you can do nothing. At least, such is the common opinion.

Now, I tell you without fear of being mistaken, that notion is false—absolutely false.

Of course when we are young we have the face which we have, and it is scarcely possible to make any change in it. But as we grow older, we have the face which we deserve to have.

You certainly know some persons in their forties whose features are regular and well proportioned. However, their face is insipid and expressionless, without charm, without attractiveness.

On the other hand, there are others, quite ill-favored from the physical point of view, who possess a mysterious beauty. It is as if an interior light illumined their features to correct them and give them charm.

In his celebrated work, *Man the Unknown*, Alexis Carrel explains this phenomenon thus: "The shape of the face, of the mouth, of the cheeks, of the eyelids and all the other features of the countenance are determined by the habitual position of the flat muscles which move under the skin.

"And the position of these muscles depends on the condition of our thoughts. Certainly everyone can change his facial expression at will, but he does not keep this mask permanently.

"Unknown to us, the face is modeled on the state of our conscience. As we grow older it becomes the more and more exact image of the sentiments, the appetites, and the aspirations of our entire being.

"The beauty of a young man is the consequence of the natural harmony of his features. The rare beauty of an old man reveals the condition of his soul."

These words of Carrel explain how a person who strives to develop in himself mercy, kindness, understanding, and purity acquires little by little a great spiritual beauty which is reflected in his face.

With all due deference to Helena Rubinstein and her competitors, the best beauty aids are the positive virtues.

Yes, we shall end with having the face we deserve!

AN UNFORTUNATE MAN

Indeed, he was truly an unfortunate. First of all, he was the victim of a surgical error—an error which might occur once in a million times at most.

On the operating table, as a consequence of a faulty technique or a distraction, the surgeon removed his good kidney instead of the diseased one.

When informed of this situation, the man turned to God and made a rather astonishing comment: "Lord," he said, "You are very contrary, but since I cannot change You, I shall take You as You are."

This somewhat grumbling remark, so touching in its loving resignation, the poor unfortunate man—one of my confrères, a Dominican priest—would later have occasion to use many times.

One evening, for instance, he wanted to take some medicine to ease a cough which was preventing him from sleeping. Feeling around in his little medicine chest, he made a mistake and drank instead of the cough medicine, tincture of iodine.

Vigorous treatment saved him, providentially.

At another time (again it was night), the Father was returning from a sick-call to a dying man. And in order not to disturb the sleep of his confrères, he took off his shoes at the foot of the stairs.

A misfortune—yet another!—was slyly lying in wait for him. The poor man missed the top step. He stumbled, and his shoes proceeded to strike violently against the Father Prior's door.

It was in such circumstances that he liked to repeat, "Lord, You are very contrary, but since I cannot change You, I will take You as You are."

* * *

This dear unfortunate priest died on Christmas Day, 1947.

I do not doubt the kindly welcome the Lord reserved for him. His Master must have said to him : "Come, good and faithful servant. You took Me as I was. In my turn, I take you as you are. Your misfortunes are over. Be happy forever!"

II

Cultivate Hope

NEVER DESPAIR

Let's admit it: we permit discouragement to undermine our strength and our hopes too quickly.

In too many circumstances we lower the flag; we surrender even before the battle has really begun. The first lack of success casts us to the ground. Instead of getting up and resuming the struggle, we accept defeat. What a shame!

In most cases to hold out a month longer, a week longer, perhaps even a day longer would have changed everything. Instead of lamenting a defeat, we could have celebrated a victory.

* * *

A few days ago at the radio station, I met a reformed drunkard whose life illustrates marvelously well our topic today.

Here is the story that he will tell you in a few words, supporting the facts with proofs.

He lived in an almost constant state of intoxication from the age of eighteen years to the age of twenty-seven.

We can scarcely believe to what a state of dereliction such a vice can lead its victim. For want of something better he would even drink "anti-freeze"; he would drink the alcohol which he extracted by risky methods from shoe polish.

One morning the poor man woke up in a hotel room in Toronto, without knowing how or why he had left Montreal.

And this is only one example, among hundreds of others, of his misadventures—each more tragic than the other.

He went from pranks to disgraceful deeds, and finally came under the care of a psychiatrist in the prison in Bordeaux. Distinguished specialists had just declared him incurable when the advocates of AA (Alcoholics Anonymous) decided to try to pull him out of the mire. For two long years these Good Samaritans devoted themselves to the task without letting failures or relapses lessen their confidence.

At last their perseverance was rewarded. In fact, since the 15th of April, 1949, the former drunkard has not taken a single drop of alcoholic drink.

"In spite of many opportunities," he said to me proudly, "in spite of a permanent temptation which doubtless will never disappear, I am holding firmly, without the least break, to my promise. I thank God."

What would have happened if the AA had abandoned their project a few days before the 15th of April, 1949? Would not victory have eluded them?

Fortunately, they persisted.

Is there a better illustration of the principle: "We must never despair"?

LET US BLOOM WHERE GOD HAS PLANTED US

"We must bloom where God has planted us."

I have known for a long time the wisdom and force of this maxim which Saint Francis de Sales loved to repeat.

However, I never realized the practical value of it so well as on the occasion of a visit to the Cardinal Léger Hospital in Montreal.

A series of providential circumstances brought me in contact with a twenty-three-year-old patient who was paralyzed from infancy with a peculiar disease of the spine. His condition became increasingly worse until he had to remain permanently in bed flat on his stomach continuously at least twenty-two hours out of every twenty-four.

Will you believe this? I have seldom met anyone so calm, so happy. His whole person radiates profound serenity.

Here is someone who grows and blooms in spite of the aridity of the soil in which God has planted him.

The Chaplain of the hospital disclosed to me a fact in regard to this patient which I consider overwhelming.

It is he, this permanent invalid, bed-ridden as he is, who raises the morale of many patients.

How does he come in contact with them when his illness confines him to his room?

Here is his secret. This young man with the apostolic heart manages to edit bulletins which are afterward duplicated and distributed throughout the entire hospital.

I have read these bulletins. All appeared to me clear,

informative, and morally enlightening. Each one contained messages of comfort and hope.

The other day when I was leaving this courageous Christian, when his calm eyes were bidding me a smiling "good-bye," I resolved to say to you: "Let us, you and I, stop complaining of our childish hurts; let us try like this paralytic to 'bloom where God has planted us.'"

MAKE THE BEST OF THINGS

I advise you to inscribe this maxim in letters of gold on your soul. May it inspire you how to react whenever life imposes on you those trials which I should call inevitable, fatal, or necessary.

Here you are with a misfortune which clings to you and which you are not able to shake off in any way. What attitude are you going to take?

I suggest that you imitate two of my friends, genuine princes in the realm of optimism.

* * *

You will never forget the first of these if you happen to meet him.

Since the amputation of two legs and an arm some ten years ago, he has pushed himself around in a wheel chair.

Now, I think I have never met anyone so jovial. He is always ready with a joke. His conversation sparkles like the best champagne.

Your first impulse is to sympathize with a man who,

at first glance, appears so handicapped. On the contrary, it is you who on leaving him, will be cheered up, comforted, and more of an optimist. How can you not admire this good man when he says to you: "God is truly the good God. Ah, yes! He was so good as to leave me my better arm—my right arm."

Isn't this way of acting worth more than all the simpering self-pity in the world? Besides, groaning, weeping, protesting, revolting will avail nothing. On the contrary, they only make matters worse. In reality, complaints and whining repel persons, while gaiety attracts them.

My crippled friend is victorious on all counts.

* * *

So it is with another of my good friends, who cannot see.

His blindness is incurable. His eyes are withered and his eyelids are closed, as if sewed over the cavities.

Now, this man, too, has a warm greeting for everybody. As for me, after each of our meetings, I leave with a firm conviction that life truly is worth living.

The most astonishing thing, is, perhaps, that his optimism has transformed such a serious handicap into a sense of well-being.

One day I dared to ask him: "If, against all possibility, someone would offer to restore your sight, would you accept?" Without a second's hesitation, he answered, "Frankly, I would prefer to remain blind. You see, I am at ease in my interior world, whose riches I have learned little by little to appreciate. I am sure that few of those who can see enjoy the charms of music as much as I do.

31

And that is only one source of my joy. Be assured I would not change my lot for anything in the world."

*　　*　　*

Like my two friends, the cripple and the blind man, let us try to make the best of things. In that way, during all our lives we shall convert minus signs into plus signs —our privations into privileges.

Oh! I know we shall not succeed overnight. All the more reason to begin right away.

YOU ARE THE ARCHITECT OF YOUR OWN HAPPINESS

Recall the great moments of your life. Analyze the cause of your sadness and your joys. Observe your relatives and your friends. See what makes them happy and unhappy.

Such an investigation, even short and superficial, will lead you to admit the wisdom contained in today's capsule: "We make our own happiness from within, much as the bee makes honey."

Isn't it true that your deepest joys depended less on external circumstances than on a certain quality of soul, a certain positive and Christ-like attitude which you had in regard to persons and things?

Does not the experience of others confirm yours?

You are certainly acquainted with some of these persons favored by fortune, of whom we say that they have everything to make them happy. And yet at times their confidences reveal to us depths of sadness in their troubled hearts.

On the contrary, you often meet among the least favored persons gushing springs of joy and optimism.

Think of those radiant persons whom I mentioned in these last few *Capsules*. Think of the cripple, deprived of two legs and an arm, whose laugh rings out like a silver trumpet; think of the paralytic whose duplicated messages circulate through the hospital of Saint Charles Borromeo like swallows bringing hope. Think of the man blind from birth who succeeded in making the best of his condition and transformed his darkness into pillars of fire.

How many others like them have a thousand good reasons for complaining! See them react in a positive way and create, as it were, a continuous fountain of hope.

These are so many proofs that "we make our own happiness from within as the bee makes honey."

* * *

Just one brief remark before I conclude.

You must know that I am neither naïve enough, nor blind enough, nor visionary enough to maintain that we can transform this earth into a new terrestrial paradise. No magic process will ever relieve human life of trials, tedium, and vexations.

There are, however, some recipes for preparing oneself to sustain the weight of living; recipes for seeing the beautiful side of things, of persons, and events; recipes to remind everyone that the blackest clouds have their silver linings.

In short, there are recipes for acquiring optimism, and it is these prescriptions that I am giving you in the form of capsules.

AT THE LATEST...DAY AFTER TOMORROW

"A check for five dollars causes the death of five persons."

Such was the news published recently in big headlines in a local newspaper of a mining town in these United States.

Exactly what had happened? Well here is the story. A certain miner had been able to get work only one day that week. Now, his pay check, less the ordinary deductions, amounted to only five dollars. In a gesture of complete despair he killed his wife and three children and then committed suicide.

The maddening part of the whole affair is that shortly after the tragedy, the mine resumed full time operations and reimbursed all the employees for the time lost.

* * *

How many times have we been tempted to think that all is over; all our horizons lost; all our roads blocked; all our hopes vain. On these occasions we have the impression of being caught in a trap from which we can never escape.

Of course, there is no danger that in such circumstances we shall imitate the miner in his passionate folly. But our courage can diminish and we may risk making decisions which we shall regret.

34

Let us not act harshly; let us rally—even while in the trough of the wave—let us reason:

(1) That the situation is seldom as terrible as it appears to the eyes of a pessimist. Even the darkest cloud has its silver fringe.

(2) That there are always within us unexplored sources of energy. While there is life, there is hope.

TOO NAÏVE?

I imagine that with my *Capsules of Optimism* I must appear to some to be lacking in realism. Doubtless, they think: "The good Father—what a dreamer, what a guileless man, what a dispenser of myths!"

My answer will be quite simple.

I believe with all my heart in the good news of salvation brought by Jesus; I believe with all my heart in the generative power of happiness as found in the loyal application of the Gospel formula: "Love one another."

Yes, I believe love of neighbor is the best way to be happy and to make others happy.

Do not tell me that the world is wicked; that we can do nothing about it. That would be a poor excuse.

I tell you that even among wicked men there is a depth of kindness. Speak to such a man—hard, exacting, pitiless—of his mother, of his little children, of his favorite pastime, you will see him grow tender, become amiable.

Yes, there is good in the human heart.

Ask some stranger whom you meet on the street for a

light for your cigarette, he will eagerly render this slight service.

Did you ever happen to lose your way in a strange city? Isn't it true that the first person who comes along willingly gives you the information you need to put you on the right road?

I saw this same natural kindness shown the other day when a minor accident had occurred. As the result of a wrong maneuver, a station wagon had overturned completely on its side. Immediately two men sprang out, from I know not where, and helped the driver out of the car. Then, in a few minutes about fifteen other volunteers had righted the car.

Yes, there is good in the human heart.

Let us imitate our Lord Who always addressed Himself to what is best in man. By our kindness, our gaiety, our helpfulness, let us assist those around us to develop their good qualities.

Without denying the existence of evil, let us restrict its influence by working, each in our own small sector, to make the world a better and happier place.

PROVIDENCE—NOT DEATH!

In the course of the last World War, an American plane came down in the Pacific Ocean. The crew had barely enough time before it sank to get into two small rubber boats. Among them was Captain Rickenbacker who later became President of Eastern Air Lines.

Now, Rickenbacker is a good Christian and it was

at his suggestion that they decided to read some passages from the New Testament at a fixed time every day.

The evening arrived when the last rations of food were exhausted; even the last reserves of fresh water were gone. That very evening when nothing remained, they came upon the passage of the Gospel in which Jesus said: "Do not be anxious . . . Your Father in Heaven knows what you need. Seek first His Kingdom and all these things will be given to you."

Such words in such circumstances must have seemed a tragic irony.

However, a few minutes later a sea gull swooped down, as if by miracle, and perched on Rickenbacker's cap. He seized it, dismembered it and distributed it to his companions in misfortune. And this unexpected food helped them to hold out until the arrival of help twenty-four hours later, just nineteen days after the wreck.

An improbable story? Not at all. Rickenbacker himself reported it in an issue of *Life* in 1945.

What conclusion are we to draw from these facts? This: God never abandons us when we put our confidence in Him. He comes to our help in one way or another, sooner or later.

God does not abandon those who do not abandon Him!

IN THE PRESENCE OF OUR
SHATTERED DREAMS

All of us, in our moments of serious thought, are grieved because we never realize our dreams of perfection. We want so much to be frank, loyal, courageous, honest, devoted, understanding, pure, charitable. And we constantly fall short in one or the other of these virtues. Over and over again, we drop a stitch as we weave the fabric of our perfection.

We priests suffer from the deviation which exists between our teaching and our daily life. We should like so much to be able to say: "Look at me; do as I do. Imitate me."

And you parents, do you not regret that you are not perfect?

For instance, you counsel your children not to lie. And the next minute, perhaps, you permit yourself to twist the truth.

You warn the young against the ugliness of impurity; you shudder at the very thought that your son or your daughter should become entangled with a pervert and accept a life of sin. And at the same time, perhaps lustful desires are disturbing you.

Since even the great Saint Paul had to deplore the existence of two men within him: one good, the other bad, how can we be astonished that along with our noble sentiments there exists a nasty swarm of vile tendencies?

However, the recognition of these sad limitations of

human nature does not justify any relaxation. On the contrary, we must:

(1) Struggle without respite against all that is less good in us; imitate the perseverance of the gardener who sticks to the labor of pulling up the weeds as fast as they appear. We must stick to our labor until our last breath.

(2) Hold to the profound conviction that God knows us; He knows the clay we are made of and He will not judge us at the last day as if we were like the angels— purely spiritual.

Yes, be assured, God takes all things into account, and because of that, He records our victories still more carefully than our failures. Let us have confidence in His mercy if we manifest to Him a genuine good will.

ABOUT NERVOUS DEPRESSION

Perhaps, right now, you are going through a difficult time.

You are just forty years old. Until this time you have wrestled, struggled, fought. Nothing dismayed your courage, your determination, your assurance of success.

Quite suddenly, you are saying to yourself: "What's the use?" All enthusiasm leaves you like the air does a balloon when it is deflated.

When you were young you dreamed of startling success. Some day, you were going to be someone very important, with an adorable wife, gifted children, a big car, a sumptuous house set in the midst of a spacious lawn adorned with beautiful trees.

Today, you insist that the fruits have not kept the promise of the flowers. A heavy autumn sky hides the sun.

But what are the causes of this onset of nervous depression?

There are several. One of them being, perhaps, that you associate a little too much with pessimists. Nothing is so depressing, in the long run, as conversations with these peddlers of the "blues"—persons who criticize everything, are dissatisfied with everything. They are always looking on the mean side of things, events, and persons.

Flee as from a plague these gloomy characters, who secrete discouragement like serpents secrete their venom.

Maintain contacts preferably with optimists—those who talk of success rather than failure, of virtue rather than vices, of sunny rather than dull, dark days.

Little by little you will look at your own situation from a different point of view. You will count up all your good fortune, all your treasures; you will think of all you have—not of what you lack.

And then with all clarity, with your great good sense, you will conclude: "Considering everything, I am not too badly off. Things could be better, but they could be worse. Frankly, I have every reason to rejoice in my lot." Tell yourself these things and look at the future with confidence.

After all, as a famous author once said: "Frequently, life *begins* at forty."

KNOW HOW TO BOUNCE BACK

"You will no longer remember this on your wedding day."

My good mother repeated these words to me when as a child I was hurt and was whimpering, complaining too long about it. They came back to me a few minutes ago.

I am writing the text of this capsule on a day in February. The sun is shining; a dry cold makes the atmosphere unusually clear; everything invites me to give myself over to the joy of living.

Just now, I have been watching the children at recess in the neighboring schoolyard. It was a treat to see them. Decked out in their caps, their sweaters, their mittens of various colors, they were running about as if to the rhythm of some fantastic dance. On the slippery ice there were falls—falls perhaps not wholly unexpected, but half provoked, or at least accepted with laughter and joyous shouts.

Two or three falls of this kind and we adults would be in bed for days nursing our bumps, our bruises, our fractures, our dislocations, and so on.

But these youngsters are like rubber. They fall forward, backward, sidewise; they fall once, twice, ten times and they get up as if nothing had happened.

They surely will not remember this on their wedding day.

As for me, I believe this affords an encouraging lesson. So often on the road of life we fall psychologically and morally. Let us learn how to get up; let us learn how to accept our Lord's help and rise; let us learn how to go forward.

And for our encouragement, let us tell ourselves: "You will no longer remember these things when you are united to God in Heaven, or if you do remember them, it will be to give thanks to the mercy of God."

Courage, my good friend!

HEROISM IN THE GARB OF WORK

There are still good people in the world.

I find proof of this in an announcement published by the Bell Telephone Company which cites three of the Company's employees.

Here we see ordinary people like you and me, whose families and friends would certainly not think of them as heroes. And yet, when the occasion presents itself, they are revealed as generous, inventive, and devoted, with living charity dwelling in their hearts.

First Good Samaritan: a Mr. Ferguson.

On his way to work he sees a house on fire; he stops; he learns that inside threatened by the flames, there is an old lady—blind and paralyzed.

Ferguson rushes forward to rescue her, but the heat and the smoke drive him back. Quickly he runs to a neighbor's house, borrows a blanket, soaks it in water, wraps it about himself and by this means succeeds in saving the poor old lady from a frightful death.

There are still good people in the world.

Second Good Samaritan: a Mr. Gilman.

On his way to repair a defective line, he sees a crowd and stops. An accident has just occurred; a poor man lies groaning, pinned under his ten-wheeled truck which is overturned.

Gilman drafts some of the curious bystanders, directs the rescue operations and frees the victim. The man is losing a great deal of blood from a deep wound in his arm. Gilman applies a tourniquet and stops the bleeding. When the ambulance arrives he confides to the care of the intern a patient who has a good chance to survive.

There are still good people in the world.

Third Good Samaritan: a Mrs. Crozier.

In her capacity as telephone operator, she receives an S O S from a mother whose child is suffocated and is no longer breathing.

Immediately she alerts the hospital and the firemen. Then she calls the distracted mother to tell her how to give artificial respiration, mouth to mouth, until help comes. The child will be saved.

There are still good people in the world!

A PARABLE

If you apply heat in succession to sand, wax, clay, a filet mignon, and some wood shavings, what will happen?

The sand will dry, the wax will melt, the clay will harden, the filet mignon will cook, and the wood shavings will take fire.

It will be the same fire—the same heat—yet the effects will be very different.

So under the strain of the same trial, five persons may react in five different ways.

Let us suppose five young fathers are attacked by the same disease—a cancer which will cause their deaths in two months.

The first victim, like the sand, dries up; that is, he does not understand what has happened to him. The vitalizing force of his soul atrophies—loses all firmness.

The second, like the wax, melts; that is, he slips into discouragement; his hopes melt away—everything appears gloomy, dark, and dismal.

The third, like the clay, hardens; that is, he rebels against God; he blasphemes. The poor man! It is as if he had hoped to extinguish the sun by his own feeble efforts.

The fourth, like the filet mignon, is cooked; that is, he allows himself to be penetrated by divine grace and accepts the mysterious Will of God. Without understanding everything, he trusts himself to the often disconcerting wisdom of his Father in Heaven. He offers his sufferings, his anxieties, his agony to our Lord in preparation for the great joy of Heaven.

Finally, the fifth, like the wood shavings, takes fire; becomes both heat and light; that is, beyond simple resignation, he adheres with fervor to the divine plan, sure that in the view of Eternity, all is for the best. In the depths of his soul, beyond the reach of emotions and understandable regrets is a firm confidence in God. He is full of peace and serenity.

*   *   *

When we, you and I, shall in our turn be subjected to the fire of suffering, let us strive to react not as the sand, nor the wax, nor the clay but rather as the filet mignon and especially like the wood shavings. Let us become a mighty flame before the Lord.

III

Make
a
Success
of Your Life

FIRST ON YOUR AGENDA

You wish to succeed and I approve that ambition. You belong to that generation of young people—smart, industrious, enterprising—whom I admire. I applaud you heartily. However, I am disturbed on your account because I am thinking of your wife and children. I have the impression that you neglect them—not from the material point of view, of course. You provide a beautiful home and you give your wife a generous allowance every week. I should just like to remind you that there are gifts more precious than money, beautiful houses, fur coats, rugs, jewels, etc.

* * *

Could it be *your* wife who came the other day to tell me in confidence of her distress?

She sees you so seldom. You are very busy. To the already engrossing work of the office, you add cocktail parties, suppers, golf—all these to increase your contacts and to improve your business connections. Your family gets only what is left of your time—the crumbs. That is really too little.

Your wife loves you dearly, but how long will that last? So many men are prowling around her and offering her the affection of which you are depriving her. And your children are growing up without really knowing you. What influence will you have on them later?

I have the impression that you are burning the candle at both ends. Stop a little while to reflect on what I have said. Then recognize your way of life. Put first on your agenda definite hours and fixed days to spend among your own family. You will lose a few dollars perhaps, but you will gain precious human values.

* * *

Why do I tell you these things? Simply that you may avoid the unhappy lot of a man about whom I heard recently.

He is already rich and powerful though still in his forties, but his wife is deceiving him; his children do not know him; and his over-worked heart threatens to play him a mean trick.

Come then, be wise! Take time to draw up the balance sheet of your life—your whole life—assets and liabilities. Do not let your bank book and your portfolio of stocks be your chief concern, but rather the present value of the capital invested—your conjugal and paternal capital. Take steps to avoid bankruptcy in this sphere, and arrange for life-long success.

ON YOUR GUARD!

Attention, young lady!

A married man talks sweet nonsense to you and you lose your head. He pays you such overwhelming compliments on your beauty, the keenness of your intellect, and your charms that you are bewildered.

Next the sorcerer tells you how very unhappy he is with his wife who, it seems, does not understand him—oh, not at all. Then moved with pity, in addition to being flattered, you are about ready to say to yourself: "Why not give some happiness to this poor unfortunate man, and at the same time, be happy myself?"

Attention, young lady!

To become an accomplice of an adulterer, to infringe on the law of God, is not a trivial thing, no matter what all the Don Juans in the world may tell you.

Even if your faith is not lively enough to appreciate the extent of that spiritual catastrophe, think at least of the temporal evils from which you would not escape. There are several; among them there would be desertion.

No illusions, young lady; sooner or later you would be deserted like the young errand-girl whose pitiable story is recounted in a little ballad which was popular not long ago. Do you remember it?

*   *   *

On the sidewalk, a little errand-girl was strolling,
At the corner a handsome boy was singing,
He smiled at her,
She smiled at him,
And everything smiled.
Their two smiles having met
He followed her with a firm step.
As he had some purpose in his plan
He said, "Good Day!"
She said, "Good Day!"
Ah! What a beautiful day!

We know the sequel. Our two heedless creatures agree to meet—and what happens was bound to happen.

Fluent verses recount it in words which would try to conjure up the happiness of paradise.

The author atones somewhat for these untrue exaggerations by admitting the tragic end of that wretched love affair which resembles so many others.

And then for the next meeting
She wore her silken dress;
The birds were all present,
But her lover did not return.
Near the pond, the willows wept,
And on the road which seemed so desolate
A little errand-girl came back all alone . . .
If my refrain does not end well,
I can do nothing about it.

* * *

No one can do anything about it. For in this way end, some day or other, all those dishonorable and guilty loves.

Therefore, pay attention, young lady!

GOOD LUCK AND BAD LUCK

At the risk of surprising you, I assert that luck, good or bad, does not play a very important role in our lives.

Without doubt, certain factors exist which favor success or contribute to failure: talent or its absence, health or illness, strength or physical weakness; however, we attach an exaggerated importance to them.

A careful and honest examination shows that most times good luck is identified with persevering effort, hard work, and sustained discipline.

On the other hand, what we call bad luck is often the consequence of laziness, carelessness, or indolence.

A certain firm has just gone bankrupt; its president blames his humiliation on bad luck; but a brutal examination of the situation shows that this man did not devote sufficient time to the conduct of his business. He allowed himself too much leisure, too many vacations, too many parties, too much comfort, too much luxury. In his case, bad luck serves only as an excuse to cover up culpable negligence.

Time after time a certain mechanic loses his job. He, too, blames his misfortunes on bad luck.

Let us look at the facts. This man has the unfortunate habit of loafing on the job. With him there is no professional honesty, no desire for excellence, no care for proficiency. His unacknowledged dream: an ever-increasing salary for fewer hours and less-careful work. Like the bankrupt president, "bad luck" is the alibi by which he tries to camouflage his negligence and indolence.

It is not my intention even to think of belittling the condition of the really unfortunate. There are many such, I admit, and they have always had my deepest sympathy.

I maintain only that ordinarily the lucky ones are those who work hard, long, and perseveringly.

Let us manage then, to belong to this category of lucky ones!

HOW TO PREPARE FOR A
HAPPY MARRIAGE

I was substituting one evening for a lecturer who was giving a course on "The Duty of Preparation for Marriage." I was quite familiar with my subject, "The Choice of a Partner."

However, as I enumerated the conditions necessary for a good choice—conditions which are necessary for a happy marriage, I saw several faces darken.

At the end of the lecture I had a distinct impression that a good half of the couples present began to realize that they were making a mistake in their choice.

Were they going to have the courage to separate in order to find a more suitable companion? I doubted it. They were already too far along the road leading to an unhappy marriage.

We can never sufficiently counsel young people to open their eyes before their hearts are blinded. From their first meeting, they should, as far as possible, make a study of all the relevant factors. If they find too great a divergence in their habits of thinking, let them separate immediately, before it is too late.

Indeed, in order to bring about a successful marriage, you must set out with a handful of trumps: physical attraction, certainly, but also—and especially—the knowledge that you think alike on all the important goals of life.

After marriage, these young people will otherwise seek in vain to realize a complete sexual harmony; their household will be managed indifferently if their views are too dissimilar in regard to their manner of serving God, of administering the finances, of spending their leisure, of planning their families, etc.

In Japan, most marriages are arranged without consulting the future spouses.

The parents confide to an intimate friend of the family the task of finding a good husband for their daughter. After inquiries, consultations, deliberations, the friend recommends a young man who, in his opinion—based on the similarity of social standing, breeding, education, tastes, and aptitudes—is most suitable.

Then, if the parents on both sides are in agreement, the young people meet once or twice and the marriage takes place. Usually it is a success.

There, as a general rule, love comes after marriage. Here, on the contrary, all too often, love vanishes after marriage.

To help to correct this situation in our country, the young people must not misuse their liberty of choice by depending, for example, on physical qualities alone.

To begin with, they must not look for a sort of lover or mistress—lawful, of course—but let them seek above all a lifetime companion.

Their chance for a successful marriage will be so much the greater.

TO YOU, NEWLYWEDS!

Take time! Save! Buy for cash and you will get twice as much for your money.

That is the excellent advice which Marcelle Auclair and her husband put into practice at the beginning of their married life.

Let me tell you about Marcelle Auclair, the well-known Parisian journalist. She is wealthy now and so is her husband.

This was not so when as newlyweds they lived in a single little room and took only one meal out of every two. To add to their budget while they were students, they accepted various jobs. One such job was the preparation of advertising material for a pharmaceutical company. Among the medicines to be advertised was a remedy for colds which was completely unknown to them. However, they praised it so convincingly that at the first symptoms of the flu they bought a bottle for themselves.

In recalling these memories, Marcelle Auclair confesses, with a twinge of nostalgia, that they were "the good old days."

You, as well as I, know some young couples who give proof of courage and wisdom by not beginning their married life head over heels in debt.

They prefer to do without things now in order to make the future more secure. So, little by little, they furnish their homes as the money becomes available.

I congratulate them for having enough good sense to follow the advice I gave at the beginning:

Take time! Save! Buy for cash and you will get twice as much for your money!

WE CAN ALWAYS BREAK OUR CHAINS

"I am made that way!"

Such is the poor excuse we give ourselves when we have not enough courage to correct our faults or our vices.

*   *   *

One man flies into a rage because of a "yes" or a "no," and he terrifies his wife and children.

Another spends all his earnings on drink and for this reason he and his family are forced to live in a hovel.

A third is jealous and tyrannizes his wife, though the poor woman never had the least idea of being unfaithful to him.

Invite these characters to reform. Nine chances out of ten, they will answer: "I am made that way."

Come now, there is always a way to become better when you are willing and, at the same time, ask God's help.

Note that no one appears so resigned to fate in other spheres.

The diabetic does not wait for death with his arms folded, sighing: "Alas, I am made that way."

The cripple drags himself along on crutches.

The blind man learns Braille.

The heart patient slackens his pace.

In the physical order then, everybody seeks to improve his lot. No one believes in an inexorable fate.

Why do we reserve for the moral order alone that lazy and deplorable excuse: "I am built like that. There is nothing I can do about it"?

On the contrary, there is something that can be done about it.

Let the irascible, the everlastingly furious man work at taming his temper. With energy and practice he will attain that gentleness that Jesus has made one of His Beatitudes.

Let the drunkard enroll with the "Alcoholics Anonymous." Like so many others he will become sober again.

Let the jealous man reason with himself. If need be, let him ask a friend for a helping hand.

* * *

Help yourself, my friend, and Heaven will help you. You and yours will be so much happier.

Courage!

SLEEP SOUNDLY

Do you get up in the morning in ill-humor, in bad spirits, tongue thick, your whole body stiff?

Well then, look to it—and as soon as possible. Perhaps very little will be needed to change the situation completely and you will begin your day with a mind eager, alert, clear, and with your body in excellent condition.

I know a man who spent the first hours of the morning in a sort of fog. He woke up by zones ... beginning with his feet. Not until about ten o'clock in the morning did his head emerge from the mists of sleep. Without realizing it, he was suffering from a liver complaint. At last he consulted a doctor; a very simple remedy was prescribed and now, restored to normalcy, my friend rises at the first sound of the alarm clock.

Some persons get up grumbling, disagreeable, impatient, from other causes equally commonplace, and which can just as easily be corrected: an uncomfortable mattress, a badly aired bedroom, too heavy suppers, a snack just at bedtime, and the like. If such is your case, confront the situation squarely and impose on yourself the necessary sacrifices. You will be rewarded a hundred-fold, for your sleep will become refreshing and invigorating.

Perhaps you belong to a different class of poor sleepers. Perhaps, you take your problems, your fears, and your anxieties to bed with you.

Your long experience should have taught you that you settle nothing during these minutes and even hours of wakefulness.

It is well to drop your cares when you drop your clothing. Place them all at the foot of your bed. You will sleep so much better.

On awaking rested, you will more readily find the best solution to your problems.

The night will give you counsel. Yes, but only on condition that you sleep then.

Jesus Himself said: "Sufficient for the day is the evil thereof."

Keep this in mind!

CORK OR COMPASS?

Are you a cork floating on the water? Do you go to the right, left, up, down, according to the currents, the influences, the pressures? Are you tired of this state of affairs? Do you want to take the direction of your life in hand? Do you want to advance toward God; toward the majestic meeting with Him in the evening of your life, with a firm step, without stumbling? Do you want to follow the straightest line possible?

From many recipes, I propose one; it is very unpretentious but most efficacious.

Here it is: Strengthen your will. Impose upon yourself the doing of one or two things which you do not like to do, simply because you do not like to do them.

For instance, after a meal you like to have a cigarette. Once in awhile then, simply to mortify your whim, do not smoke.

You enjoy a drink of soda in the afternoon. Simply to overcome your impulses, drink a big glass of water instead.

You receive a letter which you have been expecting for a long time. Check your impatience by a delay of two minutes before reading it, simply to prove that you are not a slave to your curiosity.

Profit in this way from the thousand occasions which everyday life presents to exercise self-control. For example, once in awhile:

—Get up at the first sound of your alarm clock.

—Repress your anger when your shoelace stubbornly remains knotted.

And so on.

So many little victories over whims, indolence, negligence, carelessness and also over impatience, bad humor, and anger are like an investment of energy from which you will receive considerable interest.

Your will will emerge stronger, more vigorous, all ready to win great victories when the occasion presents itself.

You will resemble not a cork on the waters, but a compass directed to God.

TODAY, LET US CONCERN OURSELVES WITH TODAY

A squirrel.

His cage spins around.

The squirrel runs at a furious gait.

The cage turns more quickly, still more quickly.

Results: nothing.

In fact at the end of five minutes of frantic running, the squirrel finds himself in exactly the same spot. He has not advanced an inch.

So it is with us when we worry excessively about the future.

At least ninety per cent of the misfortunes we dread never happen.

And of the ten per cent which really do happen, not one will occur exactly as we foresaw it.

Then the sum total of our fears and anxieties: nothing.

Why then do we torment ourselves? Why do we grieve, weep, groan over burdens which we shall never have to bear, or which will fall upon our shoulders in some unexpected way?

Let us wait; let us reserve our strength! When these times come, we shall have need of all our strength to find the suitable solutions and to apply them. Day by day let us solve our problems.

This is what Jesus said in the Our Father.

"Give us this day our daily bread."

If you gave us today, Lord, bread for tomorrow and the next day, all would be stale when we went to eat it.

Sufficient for the day are its sorrows; sufficient for the day, its joys.

Nothing prevents you, of course, from glancing at the future. Nothing prevents you from quickly considering possible solutions for possible problems.

But all this on one condition: that is, that you reserve the greater part of your energy for the present.

The present is the only period of time over which we have full power.

The past? It has slipped away from us.

The future? It is not yet ours to control.

There remains the present. Just think! We *can* have an effect on that; we can make it great and beautiful; we can fill it with love of God and of neighbor.

Let us stamp each minute which passes with living charity.

Come on, then! To work!

NOTHING FOR NOTHING

"Oh, how lucky they are! They are successful in everything!" we sometimes say of certain persons.

Come now!

With very rare exceptions, those who succeed are, above all, intense workers, tenacious, disciplined, and daring.

What we call their luck they make for themselves with sweat, dark circled eyes, stiff muscles, bleeding, and nausea.

In the end they discover luck by rushing headlong against routine, against spider-webs, against obsolete ideas, against great hazards.

The so-called lucky ones hack out a road as with an ax, chopping away laziness, indolence, and idleness.

They are sincere, upright, proud, confident and, with eyes aglow, they do not allow themselves to be held back by "wait," "perhaps," "sometimes," "who knows."

They go forward.

Right here at the radio station, I see people who are succeeding at that price—who are making their own luck.

The studio indeed has the air of a beehive. Each one comes and goes, devoting himself to the task of the moment, a hundred per cent of professional integrity, a hundred per cent of ingenuity, a hundred per cent of youthful spirit, a hundred per cent of joyful dedication.

Well then, you can understand that if a lazy fellow dared to attribute the success of the station to luck, I would laugh at him.

Luck does not explain every success—far from it. What counts ultimately is work and perseverance.

Well then, roll up your sleeves!

IS CRIME A DISEASE?

Man's knowledge of science is progressing with the steps of a giant in his seven-league boots, and we must be glad about that.

Distinguished scholars observe, as it were in a microscope, the behavior of human beings, their reactions, their instincts, their tastes, and their tendencies. And these scholarly studies lead them to conclusions of scientific accuracy.

Unfortunately, in passing to the masses, their deductions undergo deviations which render them false.

This leads some know-it-alls, for example, to claim that man is no longer free; that all his acts are determined by heredity, social pressures and a great many other factors.

According to these so-called experts, criminals would just be sick persons, practically incurable. Alcoholism, homosexuality, shoplifting, rape, murder, juvenile delinquency are explained entirely by frustrations, repressions, psychoses, or what have you.

Nobody would be responsible any longer for his acts, especially not for his depravity.

Nonsense!

The human being remains a free being.

Of course, all are not free in the same degree, and at the Day of Judgment God will know how to take into account extenuating circumstances.

But it remains true and incontestable that it is possible for even the most depraved to change at any moment the course of their lives.

Let a genuine good will collaborate with the Grace of God, and immediately the general direction of a man's destiny is changed. Instead of rolling down into the abyss, he begins to climb up the hill.

There will be relapses, but they will become less numerous, and the periods of virtue will be of longer duration.

No! There is no inevitable fatality, except obviously among those mentally ill.

No! We are never condemned to live in moral failure. We can always recover possession of ourselves—make a fresh beginning.

Help yourself, my friend, and Heaven will help you!

A FORCE TOO OFTEN UNRECOGNIZED

Ideas activate the world. They also influence men.

Yes! Ideas influence us—every one of us.

Would you like an example of the fantastic power of ideas?

Let us suppose that you find yourself on the roof of the Empire State Building. You admire the panorama which unfolds before your eyes: the city, its streets, its houses, its rivers. You are safe. Why? An idea protects you—the certainty that you will not fall. A mere idea, for the parapet does not exert any physical attraction on you. You are not even leaning on it.

What would happen if some evil spirit suddenly took away this parapet? Even without moving an inch you would be seized with vertigo. If you should fall then into space, you would be the victim of an idea. A mere idea—that of the possible fall.

Therefore, when you wish to reach a goal, first fix in your mind an idea of this goal, a clear idea anticipating all alluring aspects of it.

For example, you want to cure yourself of drunkenness. Think with all seriousness of the advantages of sobriety: joy and love returning to your home; the savings which will permit you to buy so many useful and necessary things; and finally the peace of your conscience.

Once the decision has been taken, once the idea is firmly fixed in your mind, go forward sure of success.

Tell yourself repeatedly: "I want to succeed! I can succeed! I am going to succeed! I shall note carefully each of my victories. If it should happen that I fall through weakness, I shall not be discouraged. I shall get up again, more determined than ever, reminding myself that Rome was not built in a day. I shall call to action all my resurces and I shall continue to succeed."

Form the habit of thinking in this way; you will be astonished to see in a short time how an idea, a mere idea, has brought you high and far.

IV

Understand Youth

AN ATTITUDE OF WELCOME

One day, I questioned a young girl, a militant Catholic Action worker, on the progress of the movement in which she was taking part.

"At the local level everything is going wonderfully well. On the diocesan level, there is stagnation, lack of organization. And all that because the President-general is an old lady." Yes! an old lady of twenty-one years!

Since the world began, there have been clashes between generations. It is inevitable.

Nevertheless, let us try to lessen the number of needlessly painful conflicts.

Then let us, the "old," the "dotards," "the fossils," welcome with sympathetic understanding and a bit of humor the critical and revolutionary pronouncements of young people.

Let us see what is wholesome and promising in their agitation. Let us think what a calamity it would be if the rising generation consisted of invertebrates or mollusks.

Bernanos wrote: "It is the fever of youth that keeps the rest of the world at normal temperature. When youth grows cold, the teeth of the rest of the world chatter."

Dear "oldsters" as we are, let us put on our best smile to welcome all that is acceptable in youth.

As for you, young gentlemen, contribute your share by making an effort to understand us. Do not be too resentful of our reserve in the presence of the "Beatles," of your dances, of discotheque music. You will find out later that old habits are not changed overnight.

Acknowledge that the world did not begin with you; acknowledge that with the means at hand we have registered to the credit of our generation some very wonderful accomplishments. We are, it is true, Lindberghs who took twenty-seven hours to cross the Atlantic, while today military planes make the jump in three hours. Be objective enough to acknowledge that our exploits of yesteryear were valuable to that era.

Our speech is commonplace, alas! But we had not the opportunity, as you have, of hearing excellent language used on the radio and TV almost twenty-four hours a day.

Finally, concede to us at least one good deed: we made you, the youth of today.

* * *

Then, young and old, please—a little more mutual understanding! The world will be better and happier for it.

WHEN THEY FALL IN LOVE

Last week one of my friends spoke to me in regard to his son who had fallen in love.

"It takes us parents," he said, "about twenty years to fashion a child into a man. It takes five minutes for a young girl to make a fool out of that man."

This reflection, which does not mislead us, expresses a profound truth with its touch of exaggeration conceivable in such circumstances.

The parents have sacrificed themselves for their son endlessly, day and night. A stranger comes along who has given him nothing; a stranger whom, perhaps, he did not know the day before, and the son falls in love with her to the point that no one else in the world seems to exist.

The father and mother obviously have the right and the duty of judging the choice of their son. If it is a question of an unreasonable impulse, based on an entirely sensual appeal, the parents must remind him that marriage demands not only physical attraction but also a union of hearts and souls.

A successful life in common ordinarily imposes a certain number of conditions demanded by faith and reason. The marriage of a young prince and a pretty shepherdess is wonderful in fairy tales. In real life the union of young people of very different social conditions runs the risk of a sorrowful ending.

As for the parents, the danger lies in opposing the newly-found love of their son even when that love holds out every possibility of happiness.

I acknowledge that the sacrifice which is thus demanded of parents is not a little one. Let them not hesitate, however, to submit gladly to that law of life written in the first pages of the Bible, where we read: "Therefore a man shall leave his father and mother and cleave to his wife."

To be jealous, openly or secretly, of the stranger, especially when she has become the daughter-in-law, is to bring about a moral cancer, resulting in grief for all.

On the contrary, to forget oneself, to collaborate by an understanding sympathy in the success of the new household, is the best way to obtain happiness indirectly. Here as in all things, is verified the word of the Lord: "Seek first the kingdom of God and all else will be given to you."

This enjoyable "all else" will be the mature affection of the young couple and, a little later, the endearments of grandchildren.

INN OR HOME?

Is your house an inn or a home?

An inn is a place where we live as strangers. The other occupants? We hold with them only casual relations. "Good morning." "Good evening." No sooner said than forgotten.

A home engenders a heart-warming environment in which it is good to live. The mother creates there a graciously welcoming atmosphere; the father is happy to return there to rest from his toil, to recuperate his strength, to dress the wounds received in the course of the implacable struggle for life. The children grow merrily there like flowers in the sun.

During a "Heart Clinic" recently, an adolescent wrote to me somewhat like this: "My father is a distinguished man; he has succeeded in a dazzling career. But, alas! he is seldom home; I scarcely know him. I envy his clients; they can chat with him at least a quarter of an hour—a half hour.

"My mother leads an active social life and is devoted to charity. Her pursuits monopolize her time to the

72

extent that she has practically no time for me. I envy the friends she meets in the fashionable world; I envy the poor whom she visits in their hovels.

"As for me, I was reared at home by servants; by religious in the Convent School; by counselors in the summer camps."

A man who had heard that letter read over the radio wrote to me a few days later.

In substance he said: "I passed my youth in a real home, and I thank God and my parents for it. We truly loved one another.

"If my father and mother ever quarreled, it was not in our presence. We could always count on their understanding and sympathy.

"We know that the discipline they imposed on us was inspired by their desire to make us real men and real women. They taught us by their example to sacrifice ourselves in order to make others happy. I learned at home that to give happiness is still the best way to possess it yourself. All my life I shall hallow the memory of my home. It was a home—a real home."

* * *

What about you who are reading this?
Is your house an Inn or a Home?

UNCONTROLLABLE!

Sometimes our optimism is shaken, agitated even to its roots, like a tree under the violence of a storm.

Just so, it happened the other day when I met a courageous mother who can no longer consider her life a bed of roses—not at all.

Her eldest daughter is at present in a "thankless" age. Until last summer, she was a docile child—loving, devoted, respectful. In a few months she was transformed into an unmannerly adolescent, disobedient and rebellious—in a word, uncontrollable.

As a single example of her behavior, a few days ago the young "go-go" came home with an extravagant hair-do resembling whites of egg mixed with snow, in the shape of the Tower of Pisa.

The mother, who no longer knew what to do to win over her child, complimented her on its arrangement. The daughter repulsed her with the reply: "That's nice! You want me to look like a fool; I know this hair-do is not becoming."

Here are a few counsels I gave to that good mother. Perhaps they will be useful to you who are now reading these pages.

From the beginning, give evidence at the same time of firmness and of tenderness. Both firmness and tenderness are as necessary as the two oars of a lifeboat.

Do not yield at any price on the essential points.

Close your eyes to unimportant things.

You must understand that the cries of rebellion often conceal cries of distress. Beyond appearances, and in spite of blustering, this young person is in the very midst of a transformation. This restless being, this disturbed child, has need of you. Help her to find her true self, to grow up, to mature.

Then, first of all: firmness and tenderness.

In the second place, patience. This period of seeming ingratitude is short-lived. If you have known how to help her through this crisis, your daughter will again turn to you with deepest gratitude.

While waiting, pray to the Holy Spirit. Ask Him to grant you the grace and light of which you have need in order to maneuver well.

Have confidence! At the end of this dark tunnel sunlit fields will welcome your highest hopes.

UNINTENTIONAL EXECUTIONERS

It is to you, young people, that I address myself today —to you whom we label, perhaps a little too readily, as foolish and irresponsible.

As a matter of fact, you are, without doubt, much more serious and more generous than we, at times, think you are. But, I beg of you, display these excellent qualities of your heart and mind more frequently.

For instance, try to understand your parents when they become disturbed about your going out at night. Try not to cause them any great anxiety. Your parents love you and because of that love, they are concerned when you come home late.

They know that if you play with fire you run the risk

of being burned. They know that the whirlwind of sensuality can carry you off—farther than you could have foreseen and willed. They know that in a few minutes of folly you can ruin your whole life.

And so, because of this knowledge, they wait anxiously for your return.

With a little forethought you could save them this anguish.

* * *

I know quite well an elderly mother who could not go to sleep while one or the other of her children—and they were grown—had not returned home. She said Rosaries continuously for them.

One night, one of her sons—he was in his twenties—came home very late.

The mother, in order to show her disapproval, yet in a considerate and tactful way, asked from her bed: "What time is it?"

Her son answered: "One o'clock in the morning."

She replied: "You know very well it's three o'clock."

And he answered back: "Well, if you knew, why did you ask me?"

A witty retort, certainly, but one which displayed cruelty—an unintentional cruelty, without doubt, but terribly real.

* * *

In these times when there are no longer chaperones, you young people must know how to avoid what would justify the anxiety of your parents. Have pity on their great love for you.

LET US KEEP IN TOUCH

I confess it is not easy to understand youth today.

Was it any easier for our parents to understand us just as we were awakening to adult life? I do not think so.

In all periods there has been conflict between the generations. That is normal.

I already belong in that category whom the adolescent rebels call the "old fogies," the "squares," the "mummies," and I imagine several among you are my contemporaries.

Isn't it true that we have a tendency to idealize our past, to speak of the "good old days" as of a golden age? Let us acknowledge it: we are exaggerating, at least a little. Let us confess, all was not perfect in bygone days. The traits of the young are perhaps different from ours, but these traits exist.

It is the same with their tastes, which disconcert us so much. But let us think: Was the Charleston so much more sensible than the Twist? And the "Beatles"! I had heard such vehement condemnations of them. Yet when I saw them for the first time on the *Ed Sullivan Show* I found them quite likable.

With a little good will, we shall succeed, if not in applauding, at least in understanding somewhat the ecstasies of our juniors.

In short, if they see we are trying to understand them, they will accept more readily the advice dictated by our experience and our religious convictions.

Young people need us and they know it. In spite of

their blustering and their revolutionary slogans—so provoking at times—they count on our love and our trust.

Let our evident and generous charity facilitate their entrance into a life filled with sunshine. Then in twenty years' time they, too, will be able to speak of "the good old days."

THE LITTLE BOY, INSUFFERABLE BUT CHARMING!

Today I offer you as a *Capsule of Optimism* a text of Alan Beck which I have adapted for your benefit.

* * *

Between the innocence of the baby and the dignity of the man is found the mystery of the little boy.

All little boys have the same desire and the same intention: to get the most fun possible out of every second of every day. When at the end of these precious seconds, adults compel them to go to bed, they protest with all their strength.

We see little boys any place and every place they ought not to be. And wherever they are, they run, they climb, they whirl about, they jump, they bounce, they caper.

Their mothers and fathers scold them; little girls run away from them; big brothers and sisters endure them; their Guardian Angels protect them.

A little boy is Truth with mud on his face; he is

Beauty with a cut on his finger; he is Wisdom with "bubble-gum" on his hair; he is Hope with a grasshopper in his pocket.

A little boy is a strange composite: he has the appetite of a horse; the digestion of a sword-swallower; the energy of an atomic bomb; the lungs of a dictator; the timidity of a violet; and the sparkle of fireworks.

A little boy likes ice cream, guns, Santa Claus, picture books, railroad trains, and fire engines.

He detests school, girls, music lessons, barbers, neckties, grown persons, and bedtime.

No one but a little boy can put so many things into a single pocket: a half-eaten apple, a rusty knife, three feet of string, a crushed chocolate, three cents, a slingshot, and a dirty handkerchief.

A little boy exercises a mysterious charm. You can chase him from your garden, but not from your heart. You can put him out of your office, but not from your mind. He is your master—this inexhaustible source of noise and bustle.

In the evening when you come home with the hauntings of your broken hopes and shattered dreams, a little boy, as with a magic wand, repairs the damage the day's encounters brought you. It is enough for him to call out joyously, "Hi, Dad!"

*   *   *

We have a Father in Heaven and we are his little boys. How could He not love us!

A GREAT MAN PRAYS FOR HIS SON

I recall that at the time of General MacArthur's death, publicity was given to a beautiful prayer, written by this great man in the Philippines shortly after the attack on Pearl Harbor. In this moving prayer, the illustrious and courageous soldier begs God's blessings on his son.

Here is MacArthur's spiritual legacy to his son:

Build me a son, O Lord who will be strong enough to know when he is weak, and brave enough to face himself when he is afraid; one who will be proud and unbending in honest defeat, and humble and gentle in victory.

Build me a son whose wishes will not take the place of deeds; a son who will know Thee—and that to know himself is the foundation stone of knowledge.

Lead him, I pray, not in the path of ease and comfort, but under the stress and spur of difficulties and challenge. Here let him learn to stand up in the storm; here let him learn compassion for those who fail.

Build me a son whose heart will be clear, whose goal will be high, a son who will master himself before he seeks to master other men, one who will reach into the future, yet never forget the past.

And after all these things are his, add, I pray, enough of a sense of humor so that he may always be serious, yet never take himself too seriously. Give him humility, so that he may always remember the simplicity of true greatness, the open mind of true wisdom, and the meekness of true strength.

Then I, his father, will dare to whisper, "I have not lived in vain."

Could you not, fathers and mothers, address such a prayer to God in your own words for your dear little ones?

THE LITTLE GIRL—HER MYSTERY

A little girl is one of the most wonderful gifts of Heaven. We find in her a trace of paradise.

No creature in the world is capable of being, in turns, so lovable and so unbearable. She wrecks your nerves, but just as you are about to scold her, she stands there before you as well-behaved as a statue—with a bit of Heaven in her eyes.

To create a little girl, the good God borrows right and left. He takes the song of the birds, the liveliness of the grasshopper, the curiosity of the cat, the cunning of the fox, the gentleness of the lamb, and to all this He adds—the mystery of the feminine heart.

A little girl upsets your house and your hair; imposes on your time and your patience, but just at the instant you are about to burst into anger, a ray of sunshine lights up her glance, and there you are—disarmed once more.

When your dreams and your hopes are in ruins; when life has reduced you to a state of complete discouragement, a little girl makes a queen, a king, of you just by climbing on your knees and whispering in your ear: "I love you, Mommy"; "I love you, Daddy."

* * *

We have a Father in Heaven for Whom we are only little girls and little boys.

PARDON, MY SON

Listen, my little one.

This evening, seeing you asleep, with your little hand on your cheek, your blond curls spread out on your forehead, I am terribly ashamed of myself.

And so, I have intruded into your room that we might be alone, just the two of us.

Just now, when I was reading the paper in the living room, suddenly I was overcome by remorse, and as a culprit, I have come to sit here beside your bed.

Do you know what I was thinking about, my boy?

About all those things which irritated me so much today.

This morning when you were getting ready for school, I scolded you sternly because you had only half washed your face; I punished you because you had not polished your shoes; I made a fuss because you had thrown something on the floor.

And at breakfast, I found fault with you again: You upset your glass of milk . . . you put your elbows on the table . . . you put too much butter on your bread.

Later, as I was about to get into my car, you waved your little hand and said: "Have a good day, Daddy!"

All that I found to answer was: "Will you keep your shoulders straight?"

So things went on.

Later, toward the end of the afternoon, I saw you playing marbles with your chums in the yard. I looked at your knees and noticed that you had torn your pants.

I took advantage of this to humiliate you before your little friends by making you walk in front of me to the house.

"Trousers are expensive . . . If you had to pay for them . . . you would be more careful." Imagine, my boy, such stupid logic from a father.

And you remember this evening while I was reading, you appeared in the doorway of the living room with a look of deep hurt in your eyes.

Irritated by your intrusion, I raised my eyes from the paper. You hesitated a moment.

"What do you want now?" I grumbled.

You answered me: "Nothing, Daddy." And throwing yourself upon me, you twined your arms around my neck and you kissed me once, twice, three times—I cannot go on—with an affection which only the good God could put into your little heart, and which only His heart could bestow with so much tenderness.

Already you were gone—climbing the staircase.

Well my boy, only a few minutes later, the paper slipped from my hands and a terrible chill seized upon my heart and I realized how selfish and unreasonable I have been.

What has habit done to me—the bad habit of complaining, fretting, scolding, fault-finding—for after all, you are just a simple little boy.

Now, it is not that I did not love you, but I expected too much from your youth. I was weighing you on the scale of adulthood, and believe me, my little one, I am grieved about it.

I promise you that beginning from now, neither my

impatience, nor my weariness will ever change all the love I have for you.

Pardon, my little one!

Good night, my boy!

N.B.—We must express our gratitude to RCA Victor and to Songsmiths Inc. (New York), owners of the copyright, whose courtesy permits us to offer this text, with slight adaptations, from *Apology at Bedtime* (Gleason-Miller-Larned).

V

Strengthen Your Home Life

PAY WHATEVER IT COSTS

If your family life is not going smoothly, if your marriage is bumping along on square wheels, do not give up, do not surrender. Nothing is as yet irrevocably lost provided you observe the following suggestion:

Put as much energy into winning back your wife's affection as you exert in order to obtain goods much less precious.

For instance, if you are a mechanic, a clerk, or an executive, you tolerate without too much ill-humor the sudden changes in mood of your foreman, your manager, your senior clerk.

If you are an employer, you close your eyes to a certain carelessness among your employees, saying to yourself that no one is perfect here below, in this world.

If you are a salesman, you restrain your impatience when your customers are demanding or undecided.

Why do you do this? To earn money, and that is good.

But isn't the happiness of your home more precious than any amount of money? Well, then, in your own home could you not be at least as indulgent, as patient, as self-controlled as you are to those strangers whom you meet outside?

Treat your wife with the same courtesy you display to your customers or to your employer. All will go so much better.

And you, ladies, what sacrifices do you not willingly undergo when you really want something? For example you fast more strictly than the Church ever demanded in order to preserve your slender figure. To be fashionably dressed, you go from store to store until you are exhausted, looking for the best bargain.

And for your beauty? ... A few days ago a lady told me that she had spent four hours at her hairdresser's. I could not believe my ears. You will never be asked to spend four hours in church in order to beautify your soul.

So it would seem that you are willing to undergo great sacrifices in order to obtain gifts much less precious than the peace of your household.

However great the sacrifice, greet your husband with kindness, understanding—and smiles.

Kindness begets kindness, and love begets love.

TACT

On that particular day, everything had gone amiss. My friend, an important manufacturer, was exasperated by it. An especially serious difficulty had brought his fury to its highest pitch. In his factory, one of the machines which was not insured had broken down, and this accident represented a loss of approximately ten thousand dollars.

When he returned home for the evening meal, my friend was awaiting the slightest pretext to release his nervous tension by a violent outburst of anger.

One imprudent word from his wife and the bomb would have burst.

For instance, this remark would have been sufficient:

"Well, here you are again in a bad humor. It seems that you can laugh and joke only with acquaintances and strangers. Here at home you show only the disagreeable aspects of your nasty disposition."

Such remarks would have set off the explosion. Bitter words, hateful retorts would have volleyed back and forth. Once again conjugal happiness would have gone to pieces.

But his wife, a delightful Christian lady, was able to forestall this misfortune.

Her intuition, actuated by living charity, told her the plan to follow.

She became discreet, silent, unobtrusive—and the claws of furious rage could not get any hold on that smooth surface.

In such an atmosphere of serenity and calm, little by little, my friend grew calm. Even while taking his soup, he was saying to himself:

"After all, it is not my wife's fault that the machine was broken. After all, it is not my wife's fault that it was not insured."

Then, attempting a smile, he turned toward the window and remarked:

"Do you think it is going to clear?"

Radiant, his wife answered:

"Outside, I do not know if the storm will continue, but here I have the impression that the weather is going to be beautiful."

And that was the begininng of a delightful evening.

How many times, we too, with a bit of good will and a little ingenuity, could avoid tempests and quarrels and put into practice the essential precept of the Lord: "Love one another."

Everybody would be so much better.

THE COMPASS AND THE HELM

Will your marriage be successful or not? For most of you, that is the burning question.

If you are at sword's point with your husband, you attribute the situation to the fact that he is addicted to gambling, to drink, to extravagance, or that there is no sexual harmony between you.

Such situations are only the external manifestations of a moral cancer with deep roots.

The cause of it all is that your husband, or yourself, or perhaps both of you have given up the effort to understand each other, of practicing mutual charity.

Since then your marriage has resembled a ship which drifts with the tide because the Captain or the Helmsman or both have deserted their posts.

Take the compass and the helm into your hands again; again assume your responsibilities with the determination of making a success of your marriage—and I guarantee it *will* be a success.

Perhaps you may not see on this earth the result of your efforts, but assure yourself that nothing will be lost.

I am thinking of an admirable woman whose husband, a sort of Don Juan, was repeatedly unfaithful to her.

The wife—scoffed at, deceived, ridiculed— employed all the resources of her mind, her heart, and her Faith to bring this lost sheep back to the fold. Nothing availed. When she died her husband had the effrontery to come to the funeral parlor with his current mistress.

Was this good woman's life wasted? Not so, for shortly after her death this man reformed and about ten years later he died in sentiments of sincere contrition. Some day, he will surely rejoin his wife in paradise.

I am thinking also of Madame Elizabeth Leseur, a Frenchwoman, whose life of devotion failed to shake her husband's atheism. It was only after the death of his wife that Monsieur Leseur was converted and became a Dominican. I knew him well; he had become a zealous apostle.

These are two extreme cases.

You will not have to wait as long as many others did.

Beginning today, roll up your sleeves; take your courage in both hands and decide with God's help to make a success of your marriage. And you will succeed—long before your death.

Courage and confidence.

ONLY ONE LIFE

We have only one life to live—only one! At any cost we must not wreck it.

Many married persons have the impression that their life is a tragic failure, is bankrupt, is hopelessly ruined, and all because they believe that in the marriage lottery, due to an inevitable fatality, they have drawn an unlucky number.

Nothing could be more false.

Despite the lamentable state of affairs which exists between you and your husband, I assert that you can give your household a new orientation; I assert that your conjugal love can be rekindled and burn as in the most fervent days.

How can that be done?

Make a radical change in your attitude.

You are presently thinking only of your rights, and you claim them with determination. Change! Think of your duties and fulfill them with all generosity.

At present, you are trying to convince your husband of his failures and to have him correct his faults. Change! See if you are not partly responsible for his shortcomings. Perhaps your husband becomes intoxicated in order to forget his disappointments at home. Perhaps he deceives you because you are too cold in your intimate life.

As for faults, there is always a happy balance. For instance, hasty, irascible people with explosive tempers do not hold a grudge.

Change, then, as quickly as possible! You have only one life to live—only one! Change, and you will soon see your husband change. Kindness, charity, forbearance create kindness, charity, and forbearance. Radiate love like the sun, and because of that warmth, your husband will soon let fall the heavy cloak of bitterness, rancor, and ill-nature.

That is a severe program, I admit. But pray, and the Lord will help you to realize it.

Your home will no longer resemble an arena where two cocks are tearing each other to pieces until death claims them. It will be a happy household where two persons who once loved each other rediscover their true love and start afresh to help each other make a success of their life—their only life.

AN OUNCE OF PREVENTION IS WORTH A POUND OF CURE

Without doubt, at some time or other, you have heard that one of your friends has just abandoned his wife and children to establish a new household with another woman. By this action he risked the loss of his reputation, a lucrative position, and many other things of real value. He took the plunge just the same, and you cannot understand his folly.

You may be sure that in such a case the drama has been in preparation for a long time. It is the result of indiscretions and of faults, small ones in the beginning, which become more and more serious.

If you had told that man a year or two ago that he would one day cast aside all his responsibilities, compromise his future—temporal and eternal—and enter into an adulterous union, he would have protested vehemently.

"What do you take me for?," he would have exclaimed. "I would never be such a coward, such a sneak. Besides, what harm is there in flirting with a pretty woman? I only want to prove to myself that I can still please them. And then, the little liberties indulged in here and there—as, for example—occasional casual kisses and caresses; they are harmless pleasures, of no importance whatever."

The poor man! He has simply forgotten that even "if the spirit is willing, the flesh is weak." In this sphere, if a married man has not the courage to refrain from such actions at the very beginning, he is almost always carried away far beyond his expectations.

Do you remember the tragedy of Fréjus, in France, in 1961?

At the beginning of the rains only tiny fissures appeared in the walls of the dam. No one was overly upset about them. Little by little, the water kept seeping through. Then, all at once, "Crash!"—the dam broke and an avalanche of water submerged the town and drowned nearly all its inhabitants.

Little causes often lead to big effects.

Ladies and gentlemen: be on your guard.

You, Sir, who are playing the flirt a little too much with some young girl in your office, with one of your sisters-in-law, or with some woman in your circle of friends—watch out! Check yourself! Put an end to these passing love affairs! Stop up the little fissures in order to avoid a great disaster.

And you, Madam, do not listen with complacency to praise of your beauty, your wit, your gracefulness from men who are a little too familiar. Refuse automobile rides, meals in a restaurant, etc., which are offered unknown to your husband—even if everything does seem very harmless. Stop up the fissures at once in order to avoid great tragedies.

For, you see, an ounce of prevention is worth a pound of cure.

"AH! THE CAMELS!"

Husbands—what mysterious and baffling creatures they are!

We see them drive enormous machines; solve extremely complicated problems; and even orbit space capsules, but they just can't find the right shirt unless their wife places it on a chair right under their nose.

Yes, husbands are often mysterious and baffling.

Capable of building skyscrapers, dams, ocean liners, jet planes, you would think they were suddenly deprived of all strength, of all skill, when they say to their wife at dinner, "Water, please!"

The faucet is a few steps away; all the children are calling for the mother's attention at the same time; the baby is threatening to put his plate on his head. The gentleman of the house sees nothing; he is thinking only of his thirst. Abandoned, pathetic, he insists: "Water, please!"

Yes, what mysterious and baffling creatures husbands are!

Their memory—this is well known—their memory is stupendous.

For example, any one of them will tell you about the home run hit by Bobby Thompson (and who the pitcher was) to win the pennant for the New York Giants in 1951.

But the same man will suffer from an incurable amnesia in regard to certain other events. For instance, his wife may put on her wedding gown and hum "Here Comes the Bride," but even then he will not tumble to the fact that today is the anniversary of their wedding.

Confess, gentlemen, that what you call little faults, peccadilloes, unimportant trivialities can, in the long run, be nerve-racking for your lifetime companion.

And yet you count on your wife's forbearance and understanding.

In your turn, why not grant her forbearance and understanding when her behavior seems mysterious and baffling?

Nothing will be closer to the spirit of the Gospel than this mutual kindness and good will.

DO NOT CRUSH YOUR ADVERSARY

Ladies, Gentlemen, never abuse your power, your authority.

Your husband has committed a fault. He repents; he apologizes.

Do not take advantage of his mistake to crush him and humiliate him. That would not be very Christian. And even on the purely human plane you would have to regret it.

Permit me a personal anecdote.

*   *   *

I had just finished my studies in Rhetoric. One of my uncles had the happy idea of inviting me for three weeks to his cottage on the shores of a beautiful lake, surrounded by picturesque mountains.

On the evening of my arrival, I was cordially received. On the next day after breakfast, my host proposed a game of tennis.

Now, at that time I was an expert in that sport. I thought: "Let us show this old fellow, this representative of a past generation, what the youth of today can do. I shall prove to him that we are superior to our forefathers, not only in the plane of culture, but even from the point of view of physique."

In less time than it takes to tell it, I had won, 6-0.

That victory had not cost me any serious effort. I was still fresh and nimble; my partner was breathing heavily and perspiring freely.

That very day, under some pretense or other, my uncle invited me to return to Montreal. That was the end. I had just forfeited an agreeable sojourn in the country.

*　*　*

From this mishap we may learn a great truth: that the wounds of self-love are the slowest to cure and to heal.

Remember that fact when your husband happens to be in the wrong. Triumph with moderation. Do not twist the sword in the wound. Do not trample on the fallen but repentant culprit. By every means available, you must raise him up again, since sooner or later you will have to return to a tolerable life together.

Therefore in your own interests learn to be magnanimous, learn how to pardon. So much the more since you yourself may make a false step and have need of indulgence. But do so especially because mercy to your neighbor will incline the Sovereign Judge at the last day to be merciful toward you as He has promised in the Gospel.

Therefore, show mercy to all!

A LOCOMOTIVE AND A DOG

It was a winter day, to be exact it was the thirteenth of February, 1952.

Heavy snow had been falling for twenty-four hours. A high wind added its strength to the storm and its powerful blasts drove on the thickly falling flakes which had now the appearance of a blinding powder.

I was waiting for the "Maritime Express" on the platform of Rimouski Station. Instead of the train I was expecting, a snowplow stopped near me. In order to express my sympathy to the engineer who was working unprotected from the storm, I said:

"Your job must be hard."

Without a smile, he answered:

"Not so hard as marriage."

And this man, his face ravaged by care and cold, left me with these words which were provocative of much thought.

I said to myself: That man must be like so many other engineers whom I have known. They come to love their locomotive as if it were a person. They take great care of it, oiling it very frequently, polishing its copper, tightening a rod here, a screw there, and being very careful not to demand of it more than it is able to give.

And I wondered:

Does that same man exert himself as much to keep his wife in good physical and mental condition? Does he think, for instance, of telling her he loves her? Does he think of thanking her for her devotion, of complimenting her on her successful undertakings? These attentions and this tenderness would be like oil lubricating the psychological mechanism of his lifetime companion.

It is not surprising that there is friction in a household without oil of this kind, not surprising that nothing runs smoothly.

One day as I was watching a wife knitting, I said to her jokingly: "How lucky your husband is!" She answered: "I never knit for my husband . . . such a stupid fellow . . . This sweater is for my dog."

I understand that a dog—and also a locomotive—may be more easily managed than a human being.

But all those happily married know well that the performing of acts of kindness one for the other, demanding though they be at times, and even painful, bring their own reward, as much as a hundred-fold.

A saying of Churchill's illustrates this truth.

> A painting in water
> Takes much less toil
> But gives less beauty
> Than a painting in oil.

Just so, the making of a happy home is a more difficult accomplishment than driving a locomotive or knitting for a dog, but it is so much more beautiful.

LOVE AND MATURITY

Sitting on the front seat of their luxurious car, they were driving north on the Turnpike.

Since leaving Montreal, they had exchanged only a few sentences. And already they were in sight of Sainte Adele.

A long sigh. The woman says to her husband

"This year we are celebrating our silver wedding anniversary. Had you thought about it? Twenty-five years ago on almost the same date, newly married we were rolling along as we are today, toward the Laurentides. Do you remember? We were much closer to each other then."

Her husband turns his head slightly, smiles and answers:

"I have not changed my place. At that moment, as today, I was back of the wheel."

Let us laugh at this amusing little anecdote. We must not see in it, however, the proof of a widely prevalent error. Let us not think that love necessarily grows cold with the passage of the years. Certainly, married love changes with time. Very often it becomes deeper, more intense.

Do you remember a picture published in *Life* portraying a dramatic episode of the revolution in the Congo?

In error the United Nations' soldiers had machine-gunned a car full of civilians and had killed a passenger —a woman in her forties. In the picture we see her husband crazed with grief. His love for her was evident and yet before the attack, he was probably not holding her in his arms.

100

Am I too much of an optimist? I do not believe so.

Numerous confidences and serious thought will permit me, I think, to state:

The love of young lovers sparkles, but is often like a fire of straw.

The love of old couples has less brilliance, but it often has the warmth of a good fire of anthracite.

Do you agree with me?

A PROOF OF LOVE: A CHECK?

Two ladies are seated in the foyer of a hotel in Gaspé. One of them draws a slip of paper from an envelope.

"It is from my husband," she said. "He is an excellent health, he loves me, and business is going well."

Surprised, the other lady said:

"How can he tell you all that on such a small piece of paper?"

"Look for yourself. It is a check for two hundred dollars."

* * *

A fiction, of course. But it gives me the opportunity to introduce two considerations on the family budget.

(1) The husband must try to understand well the very nature of marriage. He and his wife have united their lives for better or worse. They are associated in a common destiny. What is hers, is his; what is his, is hers. It is together they are traveling toward God.

And if we pass from these grand principles to concrete realities, we must say that the husband is mistaken if he thinks he can remunerate his wife as he pays a servant. Normally, his wife devotes herself entirely to him; for him she renounces a career; she takes care of his house and of their children; she works for the common good of the home. She is the support of her husband, his comfort, his inspiration, his companion. To measure necessary finances with an eye-dropper would be shabby.

The husband who is conscious of his responsibilities willingly gives to his wife all the money she needs, within the limits of his own resources.

(2) The wife, on her side, if she is not a hare-brained creature, heedless and frivolous, strives to administer wisely the money which her husband entrusts to her. In her eyes, that money represents the work, the devotion, the skill of one she loves. Consequently, far from wasting it, she spends his money wisely, intelligently. Her spirit of economy is an act of homage to her husband's virtue of industry.

* * *

When the husband and wife think and act in this way they collaborate efficiently in the loving direction of their household.

We understand then, how a mother of a family while on vacation could say on receiving a check: "You see, he loves me. This slip of paper is the proof."

FOOL?

No Sir, no! Your conjugal happiness is not lost forever. No! Remember! This woman, your wife—with what fervor you loved her during the days of your betrothal and your honeymoon. She was the only one in the world. You looked at her with the tenderness of a Michaelangelo before his greatest masterpiece. You were careful to gather up her words, her smiles—like so many precious pearls.

No! No! You were not a fool at that time. It is perhaps now that you are foolish! Your wife is still pretty and attractive. Look now, just look at the Don Juans who cluster around her. Come on! You possess a treasure, a living treasure, and you do not seem to be aware of it.

It is quite possible that your wife appears more amiable at a social gathering than at home. But if you should offer her even half of the kind attentions she receives in the social world, she would prefer you to all possible and imaginable rivals.

Your error comes perhaps from the fact that you consider her love as something you acquired once for all, somewhat like an investment from which you have only to draw the interest.

That is a false picture, a false conception.

Love is rather like a fire which, unless we are careful to replenish the fuel, sputters and dies out. Now the fuel you must use is kindness, understanding, tact, forbearance, humor, and forgiveness.

Come on! Shake off your laziness, your apathy, your selfishness.

Be kind, really kind to your wife, and you will be

agreeably surprised to see her transformed and become, in her turn, kind and gracious to you.

Make full use of your sacrament of Matrimony, and you will again see all that was most charming in her, who was at one time such an adorable fiancée. Have confidence.

Persevere! Put good wood into the fire and the flame of your married love will rekindle and rise high and bright.

THAT MAN! YOUR HUSBAND

No, Madam! all is not lost! I know that your husband seems no longer to love you; he is harsh with you and the children, unmannerly, ill-tempered, irritable. I know that he is deceiving you and your heart is justly embittered.

In spite of all, I repeat: "No, Madam! Nothing is yet irretrievably lost!"

That man—your husband—you have already won once; you can win him again.

Do you remember the happy days when you were dating, and the days of your engagement? That man would have taken down the moon and laid it at your feet. Now, essentially, he has not changed—nor you either. I say designedly, *essentially*.

As for the superficial, many things have changed—in you and in him.

A single example:

As a young girl, when you were expecting him—oh!

how you bedecked yourself to make yourself beautiful and attractive! Have you forgotten all your old secrets?

I know that when your husband comes home from work you are in a whirlwind of preparing supper and watching over the children. But could you not find a few minutes to refresh your beauty, to run a brush through your hair, to use a little discreet make-up, to put on a fresher dress?

Details, yes, but important.

At the same time, learn to be a diplomat.

As a young girl, you had a thousand tricks in your bag to bring him to grant your every wish, while at the same time giving the impression that he was the King and Master.

Use today the same flair, the same intuition, the same ingenuity. You will succeed better than formerly, for you know your husband now as if you had knit him. And you have in your hand the ace of trumps which no other has. You are the one whom he chose in the freshness of his first love; you are the mother of his children and the companion of his life.

The other woman, the accomplice in his infidelity, holds him in an adventure which has engaged his senses but not his heart, nor his deepest feelings.

You are the stronger, especially if, as formerly, you ask God's help in fervent prayer.

Have confidence! You are going to win your husband back again, and instead of tears, joy will shine in your eyes.

I LOVE YOU...YOU LOVE ME...AGREED!

I grant you, Madam, your husband does not know the ABC's of feminine psychology. He should know that thoughtful attentions, little courtesies, sentimental avowals are extremely important to a wife.

If you corner him, he will probably shrug his shoulders and say: "I love you. You love me. We love each other. Agreed! We know it. Why repeat it?"

Your husband is wrong to speak in that way. He should tell you more frequently that he loves you.

But since he loves you, since he proves it by his fidelity and devotion, should you not attach more importance to the reality than to the words which express it?

Listen attentively to the following story that is full of instruction for you.

*　　*　　*

About thirty years ago, Guillaumet, a French pilot, made a forced landing in South America, on one of the highest peaks of the Andes.

Noting that his plane was no longer serviceable, he began to walk through the snow, across a frozen desert. He had walked four days and four nights before a rescue team found him, exhausted and half-frozen. They took him to a hospital where they succeeded in saving him.

Having regained his health, Guillaumet revealed to his friend, Antoine de Saint Exupéry, the secret of his desperate effort.

"Had I remained up there near my plane, I would have been quickly buried under the snow. All traces of me would have disappeared. There would have been no legal proof of my death. My wife could not have received the money from my insurance for some time.

106

"On the other hand, by coming down toward the plain, there was hope that my body would be found. My wife would then have received sufficient resources to permit her to continue the style of life to which I had accustomed her."

What do you think of that man, Madam? Do you not think that he sincerely loved his wife? And yet, between flights it is scarcely probable that he kept repeating: "I love you, my dear."

I imagine that if the occasion would present itself, your husband would conduct himself with as much courage as Guillaumet.

Your husband loves you, Madam, even if he does not tell you as often as you would like to hear it.

You have the essential. Be happy!

VI

Spread Happiness!

SOWERS OF OPTIMISM

To cultivate optimism in yourself and in others, to work to disseminate happiness is a difficult task. I maintain, just the same, that such an ideal is not at all Utopian.

I remember a poster in an airplane factory during the last war.

It read:

"According to recent theories in aerodynamics, the bee cannot fly. This can be demonstrated scientifically. The relation of the size, the weight, and the shape of its body on the one hand, and the spread of its wings on the other hand, render flight impossible. But as the bee does not know these scientific truths, she darts boldly into the air and flies. And she even make a little honey every day."

There you are!

The pessimists may well try to demonstrate with pseudo-scientific theories that the world is fundamentally bad and stupid. They cannot prevent us, if we really want it, from making a little honey every day—as it were, to secrete a little joy daily for ourselves and others.

We shall then be agreeably surprised to see people around us bloom like hollyhocks in the sun.

In every human being there are depths of kindness, even in those who appear wicked, even in the most perverted.

Anyone, even were he a gangster, would offer to help a blind man cross a street. Anyone, even were he a gangster, would eagerly hasten to help an injured child.

With all the more reason, we can expect to find in the normal human being hidden depths of self-sacrifice and devotion.

Let us help develop these natural virtues by our understanding, our good will, our words of encouragement, our smiles, our optimism.

Alms of money is good. The gift of our heart in a spirit of charity is better.

After all, the practice of optimism is one of the most excellent means of following the fundamental precept of Our Lord:

"Love one another!"

PRAISE AND ITS IMPORTANCE

"Do unto others as you would have them do unto you."

That is a counsel of our Lord, and an efficacious way of practicing charity, by spreading happiness around us.

A single example:

You like to receive compliments. Well then, pay some to those who deserve them—and sometimes to others, too.

I recall that in the Dominican Novitiate, I had been appointed *"reglementaire"*—a scholarly word for beadle. My principal duty was to ring the bell to summon the priests and brothers to the recitation of the Divine Office. Knowing myself inclined to distractions, I had taken measures to be punctual. I made use of an alarm clock set for the various hours of the day. In that way, if I was to ring the bell at 8:00 o'clock, I was ready at 7:59 plus (seconds).

All went well for two weeks. But one morning I was immersed in reading when there were loud knocks at my door.

"What are you doing?" someone asked. "You are already three minutes late!"

My clock—I had forgotten to wind it—had just played a mean trick on me.

I tumbled down the stairs, four steps at a time, and I rang the bell with great energy.

At recreation that evening my confréres teased me:

"Where were you? . . . On the moon? . . . In an ecstasy?"

Laughing from the wrong side of my mouth, I answered:

"These clever fellows! When all goes well—not a word! A little slip of memory and they are let loose!"

Isn't it often like that?

We are hungry for praise. Others are, too. Let us know how to encourage them.

So you, Sir, when your wife has succeeded in preparing a tasty dish, praise her success. If her new hair-do is becoming, tell her so. Especially, tell her from time to time how much you appreciate her devotion to her home—her love for you.

And you, Madam, encourage your husband. His life outside is often hard, laborious, thankless. Find in your heart the words which will tell him, at the right moment, your admiration and your gratitude—warm words will restore his self-esteem and give him a strong confidence in himself.

"Do unto others as you would have them do unto you!"

LIFE SAVERS—ALL

"God Has Need of Men."

This is the title of a beautiful film.

It is a sublime and inspiring truth.

*   *   *

God could have done without us. Is He not the Infinite, the All-Powerful? But He has preferred to make us His collaborators.

Thus, in order to people the earth, He wills to rely on human beings to such an extent that married persons can selfishly remain childless and God does not intervene. He will not create children miraculously.

And to people Heaven; to diffuse the good news of the Gospel, He wills to rely on us to such an extent that if we refuse to be apostles, certain souls, because of this negligence of ours, will not reach Heaven.

Let us be aware of the necessity of our collaboration.

Permit me to mention an example.

In the studio from which I speak on the radio, there is a lamp which remains unlighted. Is it lack of power in the central plant? Not at all! If the bulb remains cold and dark, it is because it is not connected to the source of the current. In order to light it I have only to press the button—a slight gesture, but a necessary one.

114

In the same way, if certain souls around us remain cold and gloomy, it is not the dear Lord's fault. He has merited all the graces necessary for the entire human race. What is needed then, to brighten these souls? It is necessary to put them in contact with Christ, the source of all light and all strength. How can that be done? Most times by an action as unspectacular as pressing a button.

So it is that a comforting word at the opportune moment, a suggestion made with tact, a counsel given earnestly, a word of praise, a smile will unite such a soul to Christ Jesus.

Think of the enormous stakes for which we are playing: an eternity—of happiness, or unhappiness.

We can, then, contribute to the eternal happiness of these people around us—our relatives, our friends, our companions.

Let us not hesitate! Let us act!

God is counting on us.

God has need of men.

A VERY LITTLE CANDLE

I have just read a short biography of Patricia Young. This girl is a living illustration of the evangelical principle which inspires the current *Capsules of Optimism:* Work as best you can to make the world better and happier.

Here are some of the trials of which Patricia was a victim.

When two years old, she suffered an attack of polio which left her a cripple.

During the last war, a bursting shell wounded her seriously.

Five years ago, following an operation for a brain tumor, Patricia became almost blind. Specialists gave her only three months to live.

It was then that one of her friends, an optimist and an apostle, urged her not to indulge in self-pity because of her sad fate, but to act—to use her remaining strength and courage, little as they might be, to improve the lot of humanity.

"Only a little candle remains to you," said this friend. "Well! Light it to give light to others!"

Patricia's little candle was a certain literary talent, and she began at once to write. At first, she sent letters to the newspaper for the section "Letters to the Editor." She explained in them the Christian point of view on current events; she protested against a certain indecent film; she congratulated the promoters of a certain charitable organization; she pointed out certain books of great value.

Little by little, Patricia grew less self-centered, and her health began to improve, permitting her to enlarge her field of action.

In order to respond to the appeal of a missionary who complained of having practically nothing to read, she organized a group for the collection of old books, old periodicals, and Catholic magazines. The result surpassed all her hopes. She was able to send more than two thousand copies of publications of all kinds to different missions throughout the world.

Following Patricia's example, even should we be handicapped, let us do something, be it ever so little, to serve as an instrument of God's goodness.

Let us speak the word of encouragement which will save a person from despair.

Let us visit some sick person neglected by her relatives.

Let us arrange a surprise party for a friend's birthday.

In a word, even if we have only a candle, let us light it in order to make the world better and happier.

IN THE SEASON OF ROSES

An ancient writer, Tristan l'Hermite, has left us four lines which are worth their weight in gold.

> Restlessly, on tip toes, Time
> Steals away our beautied things
> So to warn us, "Use me well"
> And make bouquets in rose-filled springs.

* * *

Yes, time is going, going . . .
Let us consider, right now, how best to use it.
Later may be too late!

* * *

A brave and honest man at the point of death said to the priest who was assisting him:

"In my life, I have not done much evil, thank God. But, alas! I have not done much good, either. My days have been passed in dullness and mediocrity. Ah! If I could only begin again."

Let us spare ourselves regrets of this kind. Let us anticipate the moment when we shall appear before God. Let us learn that we cannot say to the Lord:

"Let me return to the earth and begin my life again. I promise not to come back with empty hands."

No! we shall not be able to say that. We have only one life. Let us not waste it!

For instance, let us see immediately how we can better practice the precept of the Lord: "Love one another."

Do we contribute enough to charitable works?

Do we give our support heartily to parish organizations, apostolic works?

Do we effectually help those of our relatives, our friends, all close to us, who are experiencing difficulties?

Epecially, especially, do we take pains so that our house will not be a cold inn where near-strangers dwell together, but rather a true home—warm, welcoming— a home where we help, we encourage, we scatter joy, where we love?

Let us hasten! Let us not put off till tomorrow! Later, perhaps, will be too late.

Let us make our bouquets in the season of roses!

SPIRITUAL "CABOCLOS"

In Brazil, far from the cities, in what they call the *sertao*, that is, distant rural settlements, we meet the *Caboclos*, a rather lazy people, without initiative, who live in great poverty.

If you ask a *Caboclo*:

"How is it that you are so undernourished in such a fertile land? Why do you not plant corn, for instance?"

The man will answer:

"Ah! Yes! Corn . . . perhaps . . . But you know that sometimes through here we have a year of drought . . . So . . ."

"Have you tried potatoes?"

"They would grow, no doubt . . . But there are insects in potatoes . . . So, what's the use?"

The *Caboclo* does not want to take any risk; he does not want to make a mistake. And he stupidly prefers not to have any harvest than to risk having a poor one.

Likewise, there are people who do nothing at all to make the world better and happier.

For fear of mistakes, blunders, awkwardness, they do not enlist in any charitable or apostolic movement; they do not give their support to any good cause. Sheltered in their little corner, settled in their middle-class comfort, they purr.

The worst of it is that their purring is often accompanied by bitter criticism of those who are trying to do something.

Those people rail at the government but they do not even take the trouble to vote.

They bluster against the parish organizations but they refrain from giving the least collaboration to their clergy.

They deplore the decline in morality and the paganization of the world, but they refuse to participate in any apostolate whatever.

These are the spiritual *Caboclos*. They are mistaken in thinking they are not guilty of any fault. They are committing the most serious of all faults: that of doing nothing, while at the same time criticizing those who are doing something.

Let us not be spiritual *Caboclos*.

Let us do something to make the world better and happier!

THE FIRST STEP

The other day I met a very discouraged man who said to me:

"The world is going from bad to worse. And the most depressing thing about it is that no one is trying to prevent this slide toward the abyss."

Isn't it true that at times we—you and I— have gloomy thoughts like this? Let us dispel this pessimism and tell ourselves:

(1) Instead of shrugging our shoulders, shaking our heads, and sighing "What's the use?," let us roll up our sleeves and do something to solve the problems of the world, even if that something is very little. You deplore the fact that our houses are becoming more and more

like inns and are no longer homes where there is mutual love. Then, do something! See that *your* home is a place where it becomes more and more agreeable to live.

(2) Instead of lamenting: "Isn't someone going to do anything?"; instead of whining all the time, let us be the "someone" who is going to act. Let *us* do something to improve the situation.

(3) Even if our field of influence is restricted, our action limited, let us act. Instead of inveighing against the dark, if we have but one candle, let us light it. We shall score a victory over the realm of darkness.

(4) Let us be convinced of the value of the least gesture. A word of congratulation to a competent professor or to an honest civic official will stimulate them, encourage them to persevere on the right road. A short letter to a radio or TV station will help maintain a good program on their schedule.

(5) Our contribution to make the world better and happier will perhaps be trifling, but let us act. I repeat, let us act! Our Lord emphasized the immense value of the mite given by the widow and the reward of a glass of water given in His name.

Come on! Let us shake off our laziness, our apathy. The shortest prayer, the least important action count. Let us remember that even the longest voyage is begun by a single step.

And so let us take the first step—the others will follow.

AS IN THE STORY BOOKS

For several days now we have been serious—terribly serious.

It is time, perhaps, to relax a little.

I shall tell you then, a little incident which I enjoyed.

Very often, I celebrate my morning Mass in a private chapel.

Well, the other day, the Brother-sacristan assigned to me, as altar-boy, a little fellow who was ignorant of almost all his duties. With difficulty he succeeded from time to time—and not always at the right time—to call out a loud "Amen."

However, there was at least one ceremony which the boy performed with spirit and extraordinary skill, that is, ringing the bell.

At the Sanctus there was a sonorous display.

At the Elevation, I prolonged my genuflections to permit the boy to indulge himself with his bell to his heart's content.

I thought, "The Lord surely accepts with pleasure this innocent homage, this unusual form of prayer."

The ringing had continued four or five times longer than was normal when finally I rose from the last genuflection.

Just at that moment I noticed two Nuns. They had entered quietly, and had evidently been in the chapel for a few minutes.

They were, doubtless, alarmed about my sanity.

As for me, I am sure that the Lord Jesus smiled at my mischievous trick, and quite sure also, at the ingenuous homage of a little boy of good will.

GOD'S POSTMEN

Letter-carriers enjoy the confidence of the public because of their honesty and professional integrity.

However, as in most groups, we sometimes find a black sheep among them.

One day, a letter-carrier, lazy by nature, found his bag too heavy and put aside a certain number of letters with the intention of delivering them the next day. But the first step on the road of negligence often leads very far astray. At the end of the year, investigators for the Postal Service discovered a thousand letters which had not been delivered.

* * *

We are all God's letter-carriers. He confides to us certain graces to be distributed to our neighbor—messages of faith, of comfort, of hope, of joy.

If we are lazy postmen, certain of these graces will never reach our neighbor.

For example, a father receives from God the commission to distribute to his children what they need in order to become true Christians and useful citizens, well-balanced and happy persons. That father, alas, can be like the lazy postman. If he wastes his salary in gambling, drunkenness, habitual attendance at night clubs, he deprives his children of what God has confided to him for them.

Likewise, a mother can through neglect deprive her children of the many good things God intends to bestow upon them with her help. An excessive taste for costly clothes, expensive hair-dos, too costly beauty aids; the untidiness of her home, too frequent holidays, occasional flirtations—all the negligences and faults of this nature impede the graces of which God has made her the depository for her children.

Each and all, we must not imitate the lazy postman. Let us distribute the messages of happiness God confides to us for our neighbor.

With this in mind because of our faith in God, let us do all the good we can, to as many persons as we can, in every way we can, as long as we can.

And God will reward marvelously the conscientious postmen that we shall be.

INITIATION TO LOVE

I would wager that seventy-five per cent among you retain an unhappy memory of the way in which you learned the facts of life. Well then, I beg of you, spare your children such distress.

For that reason:

(1) First of all, be convinced that sooner or later your

children will learn about love. They will receive this information correctly or incorrectly.

Very probably, if you follow a policy of fright or silence, they will be badly informed, for then the good-for-nothings and the perverts will take over the task.

Your children will be correctly instructed if you have the courage to assume your responsibilities, if you speak to them at the proper time and in the proper way.

(2) To lead your children properly instructed into the garden of love where they may find enjoyable as well as poisonous fruits, you yourself must have an accurate concept of the Divine plan.

It is God Who created the sexes; it is God Who planned the way in which the human race would be propagated.

In spite of deviations, the fact remains that the intimacy of marriage is noble and holy, since it is a prolongation of creation.

(3) Speak to your children with modesty, certainly, but with frankness and clarity, of those things which are in themselves very beautiful.

(4) Begin early; employ only very simple words.

If you are pregnant, for instance, do not hesitate to tell the little ones, puzzled by your changing figure, that you are carrying near your heart a future little brother or little sister.

(5) Proceed step by step. Adapt your answers to the needs of your children according to their age.

The very young ones will be satisfied with very little. The important thing is that your children have confidence in you and that they be sure that you will never deceive them. Urge them to come to you if a new problem should arise.

(6) Do not speak to them of the dangers as an ever present dread. At the same time acquaint them with the risks they run of ruining their lives by imprudent conduct and unhealthy curiosity.

(7) Strengthen their wills as you enlighten their minds, Train them to sacrifice themselves for others, to overcome their selfishness, to pray. This will be an excellent apprenticeship for genuine love which consists basically in seeking a better and happier world.

CHAIN REACTION

A few years ago, while in Brazil, I was giving a conference—in Portuguese—and at a certain point in my talk, wishing to speak of the gravity of sin, I launched forth: *"A gravidez do pecado."*

From the reaction of my audience, I guessed that I had just made a bad slip of the tongue. I stopped. Someone whispered the word I should have used: *"gravidade."*

In a flash, I remembered the meaning of *"gravidez"*: the condition of pregnancy. Brazening it out, I continued, remarking that my mistake was only half a mistake since sins, especially the capital sins, have little ones of their own.

It is true, unhappily, that our faults ordinarily have offspring.

We would be in complete despair if our good deeds, too, had not a numerous posterity.

Yes, happily, when we do good, we do not know all the good that we do.

So it happens that we say a word of encouragement and a whole life is oriented toward good. We congratulate someone and, by this act, we save him from discouragement; we give him a start in the right direction. We perform an act of charity; we give an alms, and this gesture releases as in a chain reaction a whole series of happy events.

I am thinking, for example, of this story which I read recently in a missionary magazine.

Around 1880 a gentleman in Montreal began to deposit a dollar a week for the Christian education of a Negro in Uganda, Africa. The young Negro helped in this way, married and established a Christian home. One of his sons became a priest, and was later consecrated Bishop by Pope Pius XII in Rome.

Without having foreseen it, the charitable gentleman of 1880 began the magnificent apostolate exercised by an African Bishop many years later.

*   *   *

Yes truly—and it is an immense comfort—when we do good, we do not know all the good we do.

AN AMATEUR PHOTOGRAPHER

It was a bright Sunday in June.

It had rained all day Saturday. The heavens appeared as if just washed, thoroughly cleansed. Through the clear blue, the sun comes joyously stepping, romping, skipping, frolicking, running—letting pieces of gold fall around everywhere.

In the flower garden in front of the church, a father is getting ready to take a colored snapshot of his wife and little boy.

The curate of the parish who is passing, stops and offers his services.

"Don't you think," he said to the amateur photographer, "that it would be still more beautiful if you were beside your wife and child? If you like, I can take your place. Tell me only how your camera works. Good! All I have to do is to center it and press this button? All right!"

A minute later the picture is taken and everybody goes away happy.

The next evening, the same father rings the bell at the rectory, asks for the curate, talks with him for a long time, makes his confession and goes away very happy to resume the practice of his religion, neglected for many years.

Do you not think as I did that this little incident indicates an efficacious way to a very fruitful apostolate?

At times, we would like to bring back to God some straying soul and we do not know how to proceed.

Let us remind ourselves that kindness, charity even in little details, is still one of the very effective means of opening the door of a human heart.

Let us remind ourselves, too, that in acting in this way we are imitating Jesus Himself Who went about the world doing good. Let us render service with a smile; let us help others cordially. We shall then be able more easily, when the occasion presents itself, to reconcile souls to God.

* * *

In closing, a short postscript:

The curate moved as he pressed the shutter on the camera. The picture was spoiled. Even so, it did not prevent the little family from keeping a wonderful memory of that bright Sunday in June.

POOR STUMBLING WILL!

You and I are sailing on the same boat, and both of us suffer frequently from seasickness.

I mean by that, that being poor human beings, we do not always lead a life in accord with our principles.

So when I say repeatedly, with absolute sincerity, that we must all work to make the world better and happier, you agree, don't you?

And yet, do we, you and I, always act according to the demands of this splendid ideal?

Do we not let our selfishness—savage-like—take possession of the largest shares, the first places, the choice morsels, even if this injures our neighbor?

Do we not isolate ourselves in our comfort and conveniences without caring too much about the people around us, who might have need of our help?

Let us not be discouraged on account of that. St. Paul himself confessed that he often did the evil that he detested and omitted the good that he desired. But the same St. Paul added: "I can do all things in Him Who strengthens me."

Then, if you will, you and I are going to imitate St. Paul. Pray as he did and, like him, with the help of God we shall succeed more often in overcoming our selfishness.

In your name and mine, I here recall the moving prayer composed by St. Francis of Assisi:

Lord, make me an instrument of Thy Peace:
Where there is hatred, let me sow love
Where there is injury, pardon;
Where there is doubt, faith;
Where there is despair, hope;
Where there is darkness, light;
And where there is sadness, joy.
O Divine Master, grant that I may not so much seek
To be consoled as to console;
To be understood, as to understand;
To be loved, as to love;
For it is in giving that we receive,
It is in pardoning that we are pardoned,
And it is in dying that we are born to eternal life.

VII

See the Invisible

A MODERN PARABLE

I am in the radio studio, quite a small room, lined with acoustic tile. A few minutes ago, I could have shouted, screamed; no one, absolutely no one, would have heard me.

But then, about twenty seconds ago, a technician made a sign to me and since that moment I am on the air. You perceive even my sighs, while you are in your home or in your car, perhaps hundreds of miles away.

And I, at this moment am making an act of faith, of human faith. I believe that you are hearing me. I believe that powerful and complicated machinery is at work to broadcast my message, to shoot into orbit my *Capsule of Optimism*. I have not seen this machinery. I do not even know where the tower is located from which the programs of Station CJMS are thrown out into space.

However, I am certain that you hear me. Why? Because I believe in the integrity of the technician in charge of the present broadcast; because I believe in the value of the sign he gave me at the beginning of this program.

In the same way, though on a higher plane, I believe with all my heart in the value of certain signs. For example, when my confessor says: "I absolve you," I believe that these simple words—this sign—indicates that the mercy of God forgives my sins, those faults which I regret in all sincerity.

In the same way, the Consecrated Host which I receive and which I eat is a sign, the sign that the Lord Jesus becomes the food of my soul.

And so on for the other sacraments which are all sensible signs, instituted by Christ to give grace.

I have not seen that grace, that divine life, any more than I have the machinery at CJMS. But I believe in it, and for excellent reasons. I know that the signs of the sacraments, of themselves, can do nothing. It is Jesus Who acts; it is God Who acts in them. Similarly, it is not the sign, the gesture of the technician, which broadcasts my words. Nevertheless, it is because of the sign, because of the gesture, that you hear me.

May my little parable help you to understand the efficacy of the sacraments! I possess the certainty that through the sacraments, I can draw upon the power and love of God to receive light and strength. This certainty illumines and invigorates my whole life.

I wish that it may do the same for you.

A PROPOS OF A SLOGAN

In the course of the last few years, I have employed a thousand and one means to popularize the slogan, "The Essential is Heaven."

Why did I create this formula?

Why have I repeated it "in season and out of season"?

Because I wish to engrave in your hearts the great truth which our Lord expressed when He said: "What doth it profit a man to gain the whole world and suffer the loss of his soul?"

Now if you are convinced of this truth, one of the indirect and unexpected consequences will be to make you more optimistic.

In fact, at the thought that "The Essential is Heaven," your trials will appear less burdensome and your joys more intense. On the whole, your entire life will become more interesting, more enjoyable.

You see, in many ways we resemble athletes.

"They," as St. Paul says, "strive to win a perishable crown." We believers seek an imperishable one.

An athlete—a real athlete—willingly makes all kinds of sacrifices. What motive inspires his courage?

Why, for example, does a boxer refrain from smoking, from alcoholic drinks, from eating certain foods? Why does he agree to run, to jump, to spend hours punching a rubber bag?

Why? Is it not in the hope of becoming a leader, a champion?

And it is the same in all sports.

Thinking constantly of the goal he seeks sustains the athlete, stimulates him, and gives him courage. In a more exalted sphere, why should it not be the same for us believers?

Why does not the continual thought of Heaven to be attained constantly infuse into us more endurance, more valor, more hope, more optimism?

In general by repeating often "The Essential is Heaven," it becomes easier to see the bright side of life.

ONE-WAY: FORWARD!

"Sail on! Sail on! my ship, for happiness awaits me over there."

These words from an old French song always seemed to me to be full of wisdom. I should like you also to adopt them as an inspiration to your hope, to your optimism.

You see, everybody on this earth—you and I, all of us—have to receive some hard knocks; we all must know dark days; we all must pass through troubled times.

In our periods of trial, let us think of the sunny days which cannot fail to come, if we hold fast and do not let go of the helm, especially if we keep our eyes directed toward Heaven as toward the Polar Star.

Neither you nor I ought to be disturbed by the harshness of life here below. We must not be too much surprised if the hours of rest are less numerous than the hours of work, the calm waters less frequent than the restless waves.

That is normal.

Paradise, let us not forget, is in the time to come. For the moment, one fixed task is laid upon us: to use the present hours to prepare ourselves, with our Lord's help, for an eternity of happiness.

Come on! Courage!

The port of perfect joy is no longer so far away.

Come, let your heart take over!

And let us sing at the top of our voice:

"Sail on! sail on! my ship, for happiness awaits me over there."

HAVE CONFIDENCE IN ME!

You have just lost a baby and you are on the verge of a revolt against God.

My poor woman, I heartily sympathize with you. But, I beg of you, call upon what remains of your faith. You will then hear the mysterious voice of our Lord. He speaks to you in the recesses of your soul and says to you:

"Trust Me! At this moment, perhaps I appear cruel. But later you will know; you will understand and you will even thank Me.

"You see, just at present, even if I tried to give you my reasons, you would not see the justice of them. You resemble a sick child whose mother is taking him to the hospital for an operation. The little one does not understand the reason for his mother's apparent lack of love.

"Have confidence in Me! Later you will see that all was for the best. Dry your tears; quiet your sobs. Have confidence in Me!"

Thus God speaks to you in your heart. Lend Him an attentive ear.

The Brazilians have a proverb: *"Deus escreve direito por linhas tortas,"* which means, "God writes straight with crooked lines."

Indeed, God often follows mysterious roads to reach His goal.

Sometimes with the passage of the years, we come to discover, even in this world, the wisdom of His plan.

Sometimes, as in your case, Madam, we must wait a long time.

It is only in Eternity that you will see the Lord's reasons for taking away your child.

Now, He asks you, in spite of all, to believe in His goodness.

He says, as if excusing Himself:

"Trust Me! You will understand later."

HOW BEAUTIFUL THAT WILL BE!

Nothing is more encouraging, nothing more stimulating to hope and optimism, than the description of the Last Judgment.

The Lord will say to each one of the elect: "I was hungry and you gave Me to eat. I was thirsty and you gave Me to drink. I was naked and you clothed Me."

If, as we hope, we shall be among the saints at that moment, we shall say, perhaps:

"Lord, I am delighted with this invitation to share your eternal joy. However, I am afraid there is a misunderstanding. I lived in Canada in the twentieth century. Now I have searched my memory in vain. I do not remember having met You nor do I recall having done anything for You."

And the Lord will answer you:

"Every time you have done anything to the least of Mine, you have done it to Me."

In order to understand this mysterious identification of Christ and our neighbor, let us think of the intimate union which exists between a mother and each one of her children.

For a mother, her child is herself—more than herself. The two make only one on the plane of love.

Strike the child, beat him, or simply for example, if you are a doctor, perform a painful operation on him and the mother will suffer to the very depths of her heart.

Give a gift to her child, be kind to him and the mother will be happier than if she herself had received every kindness, every consideration.

Let us remember this truth. For the sake of Jesus, let us avoid maliciously offending our neighbor; let us make his life pleasant.

Let us imitate that French-Canadian nun, a missionary in the Philippines, who was dressing a leper's wounds. An American soldier said to her:

"Sister, I would not do what you are doing for a million dollars."

"Neither would I," she answered. "I treat this stranger like a brother so that the Lord will say to me at the Last Day: 'I was sick and you cared for Me.' "

Like that missionary, let us see Jesus in our neighbor. We shall more easily practice His basic precept: "Love one another."

MY DONALDA

Have you ever answered questionnaires that certain magazines publish to help you to know if you are enjoying good mental and psychological balance, if you are spontaneously honest, etc.?

As for me, I have sometimes surprised myself in the act of cheating, yes, in the act of putting a cross in some little square when the honest and unvarnished truth would have obliged me to put the cross in another square.

Even if I obtained a perfect score, I was not proud of it, for in these circumstances, Donalda pointed at me an accusing and reproving finger.

You do not know Donalda?

Oh, well! That is what I call my conscience.

My Donalda is still better than the Seraphim. She has a heart of gold and at the same time, she is firm, energetic. And one could say that into the bargain her ear is disconcertingly sensitive and her eyes function like X-rays.

Such is my conscience, my Donalda, who tells me, "That is good"; "That is bad"; or shouts at me; or scolds me.

I have already tried to bribe her. She will have none of it. Millions and millions would not be enough to move her.

Nor will violence succeed in making her accept any compromise; any suspicious schemes.

In vain I have put her on a diet of buckwheat cakes without molasses. My conscience, my Donalda, does not play a double game. For her, whatever happens, white is white; black is black; "yes" is "yes"; "no" is "no."

*　*　*

May I ask if your Donalda, your conscience, is as vigorous as mine?

An affirmative answer, so much the better!

You must have verified, as I have, how, in the long run, the fact of accepting Donalda and her directives gives you a peace, a joy, a tranquillity, an extraordinary optimism.

You must have experienced, as I have, how, ultimately, it is better not to cheat, but to admit your faults if you have committed any. You appreciate so much the approving glance of your conscience, of that dear Donalda, even while she is reproaching you.

A PARABLE FOR TODAY

On Sunday, as I was leaving Mass, a little fellow asked me to explain the Gospel of the lost sheep and the ninety-nine others who had remained in the sheepfold.

The young city-boy had perhaps never seen a sheep except in pictures. One thing is certain, he did not know the psychology of the shepherd whose whole life is centered on his flock and for whom the loss of a single sheep is a catastrophe.

And so, I explained the parable to this curious youngster in my own way.

If Jesus were preaching on the mercy of God to the people today, He would doubtless propose to them a modern parable.

The Kingdom of Heaven, perhaps, He would say to them, is like a father and mother who were worried about their three-year-old son who had strayed away from home.

They and their other children had begun to search for the missing child.

He was seen here, there, only five minutes ago, but he is no longer in sight.

After a quarter of an hour, they alert the neighbors; then soon after, the police.

An hour, two hours pass—still no trace of the child. Then a search party is organized.

From minute to minute the parents' anguish becomes more agonizing. The worst fears take possession of them: "Perhaps he has fallen into the river. . . . Perhaps he has been lured into a trap by a pervert. . . . Perhaps the poor little fellow is dying in some alleyway, or in a ditch."

Then suddenly someone comes running and shouting: "We have found him; he is safe and sound. He will be here in a few minutes."

When the little fellow finally appears, his parents clasp him in their arms, embrace him. And for a moment, he seems to them more precious than their other children, whom they love very much, however.

"And so," Jesus concluded, "there is more joy in Heaven for a sinner who repents than for a hundred just who persevered."

Since we are all sinners, let us know that our Father in Heaven rejoices at the slightest evidence of our good will, at every one of our efforts to lead a better life, a more kindly, more Christian life.

Come, let us have confidence! Every victory over ourselves and every act of repentance is recorded in Heaven and causes great joy there.

RED-BLOODED CHRISTIANS

Radio-Telephone programs are becoming more and more popular—that is, programs in which anyone can speak about anything with a Master of Ceremonies, the whole conversation being broadcast.

The pessimists deplore the existence of such broadcasts. I should like to try to show you some of the advantages.

(1) In a general way, the Masters of Ceremonies prove themselves to be equal to their responsibilities and evidence a sincere professional integrity.

(2) I recognize that many of those who call belong in the category of everlasting malcontents. They criticize —very often unjustly—constituted authority: the government, the judges, the police, the clergy, etc.

Is this harmful?

I do not think so.

First of all, it is a "release," as the psychologists say,

for these ill-tempered persons. And the use of this kind of safety-valve causes less havoc than bombs or other violent methods of revolt.

Furthermore, this liberty to express an opinion, in spite of the harm it may do, appears to me preferable to the ban on freedom of thought and freedom of expression, which exists, for instance, behind the Iron Curtain.

(3) It is true that broadcasting errors may influence weak characters. On the contrary, it often arouses beneficial reactions. In reality, many listeners protest—and restate the truth. Others find in it an opportunity of recognizing their ignorance. Then they study and consult others; they read in order to find true solutions to the problems.

(4) I have heard at times distressing explanations of the Catholic position on some given problem. In spite of their good intentions, these stupid and ill-informed defenders impede the propagation of their faith.

Must we be troubled by this as by an irreparable harm?

I do not think so.

You see we are living in a pluralistic world, where all ideas—true or false—find expression, not only on radio or TV, but also in the midst of our work or our leisure. From this fact, the Church will probably lose those who are Catholics by tradition or routine, but she will count among her faithful more and more believers with solid and enlightened convictions—"Red-blooded Christians."

And considering everything, it seems to me that is so much better.

MIRACLES UNDER OUR EYES

We should love to be at Lourdes or at Fatima when a miraculous cure takes place.

But miracles are occurring continually right under our eyes. We would see them if we were the least bit attentive.

*   *   *

During the last few days, I took part in a Conference on Catechetics and Liturgy in Burlington, Vermont. There were in attendance sisters, brothers and priests —almost all of them young. Most had degrees from various universities, a testimony to their scholarship.

At the end of the six daily sessions of study, those who were not exhausted by their intellectual labors and the wearying heat, organized an evening's entertainment of folk music—a "Hootenanny," as they call it.

It was wonderful to see this youth, consecrated to God, manifest the joy of living by music and song. The melodies, in quick and rhythmic cadences, ascended to the star-lit sky in a tempestuous medley of sound. Between the pieces, the teasing and laughter spread in all directions.

And I, I stood in wonder as before a marvel, in the presence of the reality of divine grace in human hearts.

In the group there were young men—athletic, strong, vigorous, and likewise cultured, witty, refined, who could have established a family and been successful in a brilliant career.

They had renounced all these hopes to devote themselves more completely to the service of man in this world, and of the Kingdom of God.

There were present also young women—wholesome, alert, joyous, eyes sparkling with intelligence. Many of them could have taken their places beside the prettiest actresses in such a film as *The Bells of Saint Mary's.*

They likewise had not chosen the religious life as a last resort, a so-called refuge for morons or other ill-favored women.

And we see such vocations not only in the United States but also in Canada and all over the world.

If we reflect ever so little, we can but admire God in these souls—God who fills their hearts with His own spirit of abnegation and generosity.

Less spectacular than the miracles of Lourdes and of Fatima, vocations are, nonetheless, reminders that God is living and acting even in this Atomic Age.

RAIN AND SUNSHINE

Perhaps you are reading this *Capsule of Optimism* in uncertain weather.

Perhaps it will rain. Perhaps it will be cold.

Perhaps, you, yourself, forgetful of the warm sunny weather at the end of June and the begininng of July, are in the mood to think: "What a miserable summer we are having this year."

We are inclined to generalize in this way, especially in a pessimistic tone.

Let the temperature be unpleasant and we forget all the beautiful days.

Let us not be critical. Let us learn to recognize that we have a fair share of sunshine and blue skies.

However that may be, I am writing these lines on a very beautiful evening in July. Just now, before switching on the lights, I remained a long moment in contemplation before the star-lit sky.

A cool breeze came in my wide-open window, and with it insects attracted now by the light.

A few minutes ago a butterfly alighted on my paper. I was able to examine it with my magnifying glass.

What a marvel!

Its wings, perfectly symmetrical, are decorated with circles of pastel shades of extraordinary beauty.

How did this tiny little insect succeed in this work of art which equals in perfection the work of our best miniaturists? Where did it get the material to produce its colors? How has its body, scarcely as big as a drop of water, been able to effect chemical changes which in the world of human beings would require extensive factories with well-equipped laboratories?

Before this living mystery I adored God, Creator of heaven and earth.

* * *

I am making this disclosure in the hope that you will take advantage of the beautiful days of summer to look closely at the thousand and one splendors spread out under your eyes.

Avail yourself of this time to adore God, the Author of all these beauties, to put your trust in Him who asks only that you transform your soul into a sparkling jewel for eternity.

ALL'S WELL THAT ENDS WELL

Isn't it true that often when things are going badly in our lives we find fault with God, and in this way we reveal ourselves as ignorant, prejudiced, of bad faith, in a word: unjust? Yes unjust, for we are accusing God unjustly—and that in three ways.

First injustice: We condemn God even before we know all the facts.

For instance, we are furious because we have become ill.

Wait! Perhaps good will come from this misfortune. Perhaps it will be for us as it was for one of the most celebrated writers of French-Canada. Indeed, he owes his success in great part to the fact that suffering from tuberculosis, he was confined to a sanatorium and found during this forced leisure a wonderful source of inspiration.

How many times in our own lives, what seems to be a catastrophe is recognized later as a blessing!

Therefore, let us wait before blaming God.

* * *

Second injustice: Our verdict against God would condemn Justice itself.

Men themselves are very often the real culprits.

A man who drinks to excess—will he not accuse God unjustly of the cirrhosis of the liver which will cause his premature death?

Some young rowdies, speed-crazy—do they not accuse God unjustly if their car, going eighty miles an hour, crashes into a tree?

Spendthrifts who squander borrowed money—do

they not blame God unjustly for their financial embarrassment?

* * *

Third and last counsel in order to avoid instituting unjust proceedings against God: Let us try to understand the plan of salvation—the divine plan for the final happiness of humanity.

God respects our liberty. He desires ardently that we give Him our love spontaneously.

If we understand this plan of God's, we shall more readily admit that He does not continually upset the laws of nature to punish the wicked and reward the good here below.

If we understand this plan of God's, we shall have unlimited hope in the merciful justice of the Last Judgment.

While waiting, let us not blame God; that would be unjust. Have confidence in Him, and some day we shall be able to cry out joyously: "All's well that ends well!"

IS YOUR PASTOR WRONG?

Your pastor has just renovated your parish church and you are reproaching him for it.

The other day you said to me:

"The Gospel teaches us that Jesus, born in a stable, lived all His life in poverty. I imagine He is ill at ease surrounded by the gold and marble of our altars."

You said that, and I was thinking of the following passage of the Gospel:

149

"Six days before the Passover, Jesus came to Bethany where Lazarus, whom Jesus had raised to life, had died. And they made Him a supper there. Martha served, while Lazarus was one of those reclining at table with Him.

"Mary therefore took a pound of ointment, genuine nard of great value, and anointed the feet of Jesus, and with her hair wiped them dry. And the house was filled with the odor of the ointment."

I interrupt this quotation, to emphasize that I know your motives are very different from those of the traitor mentioned in the following lines:

* * *

"Then one of His disciples, Judas Iscariot, he who was about to betray Him, said, 'Why was this ointment not sold for three hundred denarii and given to the poor?' "

Jesus answered: "Amen I say to you, wherever in the whole world this Gospel is preached, this also, that she has done shall be told in memory of her."

* * *

Doesn't this account make an impression on you?

In it you see Jesus, the poor preacher of poverty, openly praise the apparent extravagance of Mary Magdalen.

Conclusion:

Your pastor is actively concerned with his poor, but he does not neglect the homage due to God.

In my opinion, he maintains a happy balance between two apparently contradictory virtues: the spirit of poverty and zeal for the glory of God.

What do you think?

150

AGREED!

For some time now, parts of the Mass have been recited in the vernacular. There is one word, however, which has remained unchanged, that is "Amen."

Why has it not been translated?

Quite simply, because it is untranslatable.

Up to now, for want of something better, the French have used *"ainsi-soit-il,"* the Italians, *"cosi sia."* These were rather inadequate translations which did not take into account all the riches contained in the two syllables: "Amen." The liturgical renewal has therefore retained this Hebraic word in all its original force.

* * *

"Amen" is the word the faithful of the Old Testament used to proclaim their adherence to the proposals of their priests and their leaders.

To Moses, for instance, presenting the Tables of the Law, the people of God in the desert, near Sinai, answered: "Amen! Agreed! We accept the Ten Commandments. Amen."

To the high priest Aaron who has prayed in their name, the believers, in the presence of the Ark of the Covenant, cry: "Amen! Agreed! Your supplications to Yahweh express our sentiments. Amen!"

To David, inviting them to repulse—at the risk of their lives—the terrible Philistines, the Israelites cry: "Amen! Agreed! The situation demands the greatest sacrifices. Amen!"

* * *

See how rich this word is, how precious; see how it lends itself to infinite endless re-echoings.

By saying it, we enroll ourselves in a tradition of several centuries; we use the very word that millions of great-hearted men and women have used to call out to God their complete trust.

Let *us* then, say with fervor and with pride: "Amen!"

VIII

Increase Your Power

DUPED! RIDICULED! CHEATED!

You have just done something for some good Sister or for some good Father. They tell you with the most charming smile: "I shall pray for you."

You smile in your turn, but at the same time grumbling to yourself: "I cannot pay with prayers for the food I buy at the super market."

And then the impression of having been duped, ridiculed, cheated takes possession of you.

Perhaps in your eyes, prayer appears as an ineffectual activity practiced by people on the margin of life, of real life. You conceive it as a mumbling of tiresome formulas which change nothing to nothing.

Perhaps you have had an experience like the one which annoyed the French writer André Maurois so much. As a student, he prayed that in the geography examination they would ask about the tributaries of the Seine which he had at his finger-tips. But they questioned him about those of the Loire which he did not know. Immediately Maurois lost confidence in the efficacy of prayer.

Do you not know that a God Who would be our servant, obeying us in all things with all diligence, would not be God?

Do you not know then that prayer does not consist in a mechanical repetition of formulas, but rather in an elevation of the mind and heart to Him Who at every second sustains us in existence and in movement?

Prayer is a heart-to-heart talk with Him Who is our Father in Heaven.

Prayer is an SOS to Him Who knows our needs better than we do.

If we always obtained the exact favors that we ask for, we should often be well tricked.

The philosophers of ancient Greece have already said: "Whom the gods would destroy, they grant him all he asks."

I am thinking of the little girl who saw her parents and the doctor disturbed over her temperature of 104 degrees. She prayed and asked God to make her temperature 0 degree.

Do we know any better than that child what are, at long range, our best interests?

Let us trust then in the wisdom and goodness of our Father in Heaven. Let us pray in spirit and in truth!

AN ACCESSORY!

It was in Brazil in 1945. I was traveling in a small plane from São Paulo to Rio de Janeiro. The plane was caught in a tropical storm of great violence—a hurricane—a cyclone. We were tossed about like a leaf in a gale of a hundred miles an hour.

When, finally, the pilot succeeded in making a landing, one of the passengers confided to me: "I do not believe in God nor the devil. However in the course of this trip, I said all the prayers I knew in all the languages I know."

Then he cynically admitted that, safe again, he returned to his atheism.

Are we not like this man?

In hours of danger, in a serious illness, or at the time of an accident, we cry out to God; then we forget Him; we rank Him among the accessories which are useful only at times.

We manifest a disturbing lack of understanding of our condition as creature—so puny in the vast universe —when we debase God to the role of life-buoy or fire extinguisher.

I know that in North America, our high standard of living in an overdeveloped land deludes us in regard to our true nature.

In our daily life, so many sources of energy are at our disposal that we have the impression that we could do without God.

We press a button, we turn over a switch and lights shine, fires are lighted, motors are set in motion, pictures move on a screen, sounds burst from a loud-speaker.

And what intoxication to take the wheel and to have need merely to press lightly on the accelerator in order to have a meteor of a ton or two bound along the road.

It is true that from many points of view we are powerful. But it is likewise true that under many aspects we are weak, limited—and we *are* mortal.

The most elementary wisdom advises us to pray and especially to love God—always and everywhere.

ADDRESSED TO THE GRUMBLERS

It seems that there are some persons who wake up in the morning full of joy, persons who spring out of bed in excellent humor, persons who flourish their early morning optimism as lightly as a feather.

I bow low before these extraordinary creatures, these rare birds.

Yes! Hats off!

For I, like most persons, have great difficulty in freeing myself from the mists of sleep.

Under these conditions, a problem arises for many: "When should we, ordinary people, say our morning prayers?"

In my opinion, it is better to pray as soon as you get out of bed. There is a risk involved if you wait until you are completely awake and dressed. "A bird in the hand is worth two in the bush." This proverb seems to me to be full of wisdom, here as elsewhere.

Accordingly, at the moment of awakening, as soon as we regain consciousness, before any other action, let us kneel down, for at least a minute, and offer our day to the Lord.

In that minute, we have time to recite devoutly an *Our Father,* a *Hail Mary* and a few aspirations.

I admit there will be nothing picturesque in the spectacle we will present at that moment. But the Lord, because of our good intentions will, no doubt, find this poor human being with his wrinkled pajamas, his hair rumpled and his eyes half closed, a touching sight.

You do not agree about this minute of prayer every morning?

Then, at least say to the Lord: "Good morning, my God!"

Is that still too much?

Well then, raise your hand in salute.

At any rate, do not forget Him!

ALWAYS GOOD WEATHER

All of us are fearful.

All, or almost all.

We are afraid of everything—almost everything.

Fear of what people will say, of the opinion of our neighbor.

Fear of needing money and fear of catching a cold.

Fear of the boss and of the tax collector.

Fear of the heat and fear of the cold.

Fear of taking a risk and fear of rashness.

Fear of accidents and fear of fires.

Fear of sickness and fear of death.

In the hope of quieting our innumerable fears, we take out insurance, we demand guarantees, we stop up the chinks in our hearts and we envelop our souls in scarves and sweaters.

The worst of it is that in spite of all these precautions, we continue to shiver with dread and our teeth chatter with fear.

What must we do to allay our fears?

Have just a little more confidence in Jesus our Savior. Just listen to Jesus saying as He did to the Apostles terrorized by the tempest:

"Come! Be calm, O you of little faith. Am I not with you? Certainly, I often seem to sleep, but I am watching over you just the same.

"Perhaps at times, I shall let the winds howl and the waves roar. But never, never shall I cease offering you the courage necessary to resist the worst calamities. Do your best—for you must not just fold your arms—do your best and I, the Lord, will do the rest."

Even when we have understood this teaching of Jesus, we still continue to take out insurance—but we no longer have the same overriding fear.

Let us have confidence! For those who trust Him it is always good weather!

IN THE MIDST OF THE SUMMER VACATION

It is quite possible that you are reading this now while you are taking a sun bath on a beach. Or perhaps you are strolling, reading and thinking, along some tree-shaded path.

Or again, perhaps you are in town, simply awaiting the time of your annual vacation.

Wherever you may be, even if you are far away seeking relaxation and rest, some sorrow may have over-taken you which tears your heart with stinging grief.

Is it a question of a disappointment in love, a mis-understanding at home, a feeling of dreadful loneliness —of physical illness, of a moral anxiety?

I do not know.

But if you are suffering, I invite you to pray to our Lord, to go to Him with confidence as did the sick, the lame, the grief-stricken in the course of His life in Palestine.

Resurrected, living indeed, He will say to you today as He said to the unfortunate ones of His time: "Come to Me, all you who weep and I will console you. Come to Me, all you who suffer and I will comfort you."

Go to Him. Let your soul turn toward His mercy and, I guarantee, you will experience relief, you will have more strength to carry your cross—more courage.

The Jesus who is now in Heaven is the same Who displayed such compassion when He was on earth. Remember the emotion which overwhelmed Him in the presence of the dead body of His friend Lazarus. Re-member the tears He shed at the thought of the trials which were about to come upon the holy and beloved city of Jerusalem.

It is with the same sympathetic heart that He will stoop over you and soothe your sorrows. He may not deliver you from them, but He will help you to bear them bravely and even lovingly. He will show you that your Way of the Cross must end some day, as his did, in glory and in the joy of your own resurrection.

I am telling you these things because I know very well that in many cases human sorrows do not take a vacation. Follow my advice; send a distress call to Jesus and you will experience the comfort of His divine compassion.

NEVER ABANDONED

Permit me, today, to relate to you a remarkable episode in the life of one of my Dominican confrères, Father Etienne-Marie Laporte.

He had been a missionary in Japan for six years at the time of the attack on Pearl Harbor and the beginning of the war with the United States.

That very day, the 8th of December, 1941, Japanese police went to his rectory to arrest him. He was cast into prison under the accusation—evidently false—of espionage.

In the narrow cell in which he was confined for four months without any contact with the outside world, he had nothing: no books, no newspaper, no writing materials—nothing.

On the 2nd of February, 1942, feast of Our Lady's Purification, he began a novena to the Most Holy Virgin to ask her to have at least his Breviary returned to him.

The days which followed were days of intense prayer and great hope.

On the morning of the 11th, the feast of Our Lady of Lourdes, which marked the end of his novena, he awoke radiant, sure that that day would be one of the happiest of his life.

The morning passed; no Breviary. The afternoon passed; no Breviary.

Bedtime came. Father stretched himself out on the floor, as usual, on his back, as was required, with the light of a searchlight full in his face.

Then, he relates, he spoke to the Blessed Virgin in these words:

"I did not ask you for any great thing. Not liberty. No! I do not entertain such fantastic dreams. Only my Breviary! It would have been so easy for you to get your Divine Son to touch the heart of my guards. I cannot help being displeased with you."

And he went to sleep weeping.

The next day, on awakening, he saw his Breviary beside him. He took it and kissed it fervently, asking Our Lady to pardon his passing lack of faith.

The guard approached him later and explained to him:

"I came to return your Breviary last night, but you were already asleep."

* * *

I related that incident to you in order to invite you to recite often the *"Memorare"* in which we pray; "Never was it known that anyone who fled to your protection . . . was left unaided."

LIKE MUSHROOMS

Sometimes brave Christians, fervent Christians, complain of distraction in their prayers.

Attention! Attention!

Distractions are like mushrooms: some are bad and some are very good.

For instance, you Sir, if while you are in church, you are thinking of the best way to improve your golf score, you could not call that praying. Your distraction is bad.

And if you, Madam, spend your time in church criticizing or envying other women's clothes, you are not praying either.

But a father prays admirably if the recollection of his problems, his worries, his anxieties is an occasion to beg God for His light and help.

I know a good mother who, after Holy Communion, during her thanksgiving, thinks of each of her ten children, of their difficulties, of their needs in order to recommend them to God their Father in Heaven. This good Christian has no reason to be disturbed about her distractions. They are excellent and meritorious distractions.

A few days ago, a lady was telling me of her consternation when she received the unexpected news that her daughter, a student in a foreign country, had married an atheist. "In these circumstances," she said, "I should have prayed, I would have liked to pray, but I felt incapable of it. The whole day I was like one suffocated, scarcely able to breathe and to say from time to time: 'My God! My God!'"

I reassured this good woman. Her "My God! My God!" was a prayer full of faith which brought to my mind the SOS of the Apostles calling to Jesus: "Lord, save us, we are perishing."

And I, myself, at the Offertory of my daily Mass, when I recommend you to God, you who appreciate these *Capsules of Optimism,* you who constitute my sympathetic audience, I do not try to dismiss these thoughts as distractions. Quite the contrary. For in this way, I am praying for you.

So you see, distractions in prayers are like mushrooms: some are harmful, but some are desirable.

PRAYER AN OPIATE? NO!

Prayer bores you, doesn't it?

When a priest or some good sister urges you to pray you shrug your shoulders. You think these people are living outside of life—real life.

In your eyes prayer resembles an opiate which plunges you into a heavy and disagreeable torpor.

Permit me to tell you that you do not know how to pray—do not know what prayer is.

I am thinking of that good grandmother who, though poor, reared a large family without help. She relates that at certain times she felt on the verge of discouragement. Then she would stop for a few minutes, and seated, eyes closed, she would murmur: "Lord! I can do no more. Come to my help!"

That was a real prayer, built on true faith, solid as the foundation of a mountain. That woman was sure that her supplication would not be lost in empty space. There was Someone Who would hear her,

In fact, a hundred times, a thousand times, she experienced the wonderful help she asked for from "Above."

It was, she asserts even today, like an injection of additional strength.

* * *

A few years ago I knew a man who really prayed. He was in a hospital and in spite of the best of care and many operations, a cancer had, little by little, eaten away the greater part of his face.

Truly, I have never found in any person such overwhelming peace and happiness.

"Yes, I pray," he said, "but it is to thank God. All my life I have counted on the truth of His promises of love. Soon, very soon, I shall enter into eternal joy."

And in the one remaining eye, I saw the light of an extraordinary hope.

* * *

Pray like that man.

Pray like the grandmother I just spoke of.

And I guarantee that you will not find prayer boring.

AN ISLET OF SILENCE

The World's Fair at New York celebrated the triumph of human genius over inert matter.

Passing from one pavilion to the next, we go from marvel to marvel.

Here, a machine gives correct solutions to complicated problems in mathematics almost instantaneously.

Another translates into Russian any given text in English. In a third pavilion, there is a telephone in which you can see the person to whom you are speaking.

Elsewhere, we can cast a glance on the world of tomorrow—on trips to the moon, on the exploration of the depths of the sea.

And in the evening, there is a profusion of lights, of colored fountains, of fireworks.

However, in this world of marvels, where everything seems to prove that from now on, the human being will be self-sufficient, there is an astonishing phenomenon. Here it is:

The pavilion which attracts the greatest crowds is the very one in which we find no scientific marvel, no magic trick which would justify man's pride.

There, without any notice requiring it, is observed the deepest and most extraordinary silence. When the crowds pass over the *Pieta* of Michaelangelo, those who a few minutes before were talking, joking, singing, do not say a single word. They look, and their look is a prayer, an act of homage to God.

That seems to me to be moving proof that God is not dead in the heart and soul of the citizens of this materialistic world. Spontaneously all recognize their dignity as children of God.

Facts of this nature justify our hopes for the religious future of humanity.

DIGNITY AND FAMILIARITY

There are prayers which resemble Maids of Honor.

There are others which resemble swallows.

Let me explain.

*　　*　　*

For example, on Sundays, in Church, we pray as the People of God and it is a beautiful prayer. United to the other faithful, we address ourselves to the Lord in official formulas—formulas which are resplendent in the light of the stained glass windows; formulas which seem to be impregnated with the perfume of the incense, and which advance toward God with dignity like Maids of Honor in elaborate weddings.

Surely God accepts these collective prayers with joy.

But I am certain that God is equally touched by our individual prayers, our weekday prayers, those which spring from our hearts spontaneously on the occasion of a joy or a sorrow, or even those which rise to Heaven without any precise motive; all those prayers which whirl about in the blue sky; those somewhat childish prayers which simply wish to express the intense happiness of loving God and of being loved by Him.

I found an example of these swallow-like prayers in the life of Saint Teresa of Avila.

One day as she was going to Toledo to establish a monastery, she had to submit, during the whole length of the trip, to a thousand and one mishaps.

To top it all off, as she approached the city, she slipped, fell in the mud, and was slightly injured.

Then she could not help sighing:

"Lord, if you treat your friends like this, it is not surprising that you have so few."

What do you think of that prayer?

I consider this seemingly reproachful remark admirably filled with true affection.

It is an excellent example of those swallow-like prayers which complement so gracefully those others—the Maid of Honor prayers.

ACTRESSES AND PREACHERS

She was weeping real tears.

I was lost in astonishment.

She?

It was the great French actress, Danielle Delorme.

The occasion?

Paul Claudel's drama, *The Tidings Brought to Mary,* played in the Gésu Theater in Montreal at the beginning of February, 1965.

Danielle Delorme was well acquainted with the role of Violaine. She had played it hundreds of times in France before coming to Canada.

And yet, she wept on the stage. She wept real tears. Frankly I was astonished by it—and in admiration.

An actress needs an extraordinary talent and at the same time, a very rigorous professional integrity in order to succeed in entering into the psychology of an imaginary personage to the degree of experiencing the most intimate sentiments of her being, even to the inter-relation of her soul and her body.

Tears, real tears!

Seeing them trickle down Danielle Delorme's cheeks, I made a resolution, a wild resolution, which I shall keep, cost what it may.

In my work as preacher of the Gospel, I wish to involve myself as thoroughly, heart and head, as that actress does in her profession.

She gives herself entirely to a fiction.

I have an obligation to preach truth, truth carrying infinite consequences for myself and others—in time and in eternity.

For that apostolate, I propose to call into action all my powers—absolutely all.

I shall not weep probably. But with the grace of God, the good news of the Gospel will penetrate me to the degree that I shall resemble a glowing coal, a column of fire—a light and guide to the Lord Jesus.

AN UNUSUAL ENGLISHMAN

You do not know John Fisher? Saint John Fisher?

I will confess very frankly that until the last few days, I, too, did not know anything about him.

The day before yesterday, I read his biography and I consider him one of the most admirable of men.

Saint John Fisher lived in England in the time of Henry VIII. When almost everyone in the world was bowing before this arbitrary, brutal, and cruel monarch, Fisher withstood him, and did not hesitate to imitate his patron, Saint John the Baptist. He cried aloud: "Not lawful! . . . No! Your Majesty! It is not permitted for you to repudiate your lawful wife and to live in adultery. That is not permitted to you any more than to your subjects."

For these courageous words Fisher was cast into prison.

There, in one of the dungeons of the Tower of London, he was awakened at dawn on a day of June, 1535, by one of the guards.

The guard said to him:

"God save the King! I regret to tell you, My Lord, that you are to be beheaded at nine o'clock this morning."

Fisher replied:

"God save the King! What time is it now, Sir? Five o'clock? Would you be so kind as to let me sleep until seven o'clock?"

A few minutes later, the condemned man was again sleeping soundly.

When the executioner wakened him at seven o'clock, Fisher proceeded to dress quickly. Then without being disturbed, he prayed to the Lord with the greatest calm until the moment, two hours later, when he died a hero and a saint.

*　　*　　*

In similar circumstances, you would probably not have shown the same courage nor the same faith.

171

Nor would I, either.

But is it not comforting to think that some of our brothers can rise to such heights?

I consider John Fisher one of the most admirable of men.

And you?

SAINT THERESE OF MONTREAL

You were a servant—and some hare-brained persons looked down on you.

But because of your generous heart and your instinctive refinement, you were a noble lady.

Yes, by the loftiness of your sentiments and the fervor of your devotion, you were a princess.

In the course of a closed retreat, you told me the story of your life, and your very simple words reduced me to tears.

* * *

Having become an orphan at the age of five years, you did not receive the education you would have desired; you were never able to escape from your condition of servant.

Then, making the best of things, you had succeeded, according to the real spirit of the Gospel, in becoming great through the performance of little duties.

In the help given to mothers, in the care of children, in the service of the sick and aged, you infused that love of neighbor, that charity which no money could buy.

Toward the end of your busy life, your work fatigued you more easily and you had confided to me that at night, falling into your bed, you would say as a sort of prayer:

"Lord, how good it would be to go to sleep forever, if I were sure of waking up near You in Your beautiful Heaven!"

Your wish was granted on Christmas Day.

Neither radio, nor television—not even the daily paper—noted your death, little servant.

But I am certain that the Lord welcomed you, that very day, into His paradise, great lady that you were.

So in the secret of my heart, I pray to you, Saint Therese of Montreal.